READINGS ON

THE
HISTORIES

THE GREENHAVEN PRESS

Literary Companion

TO BRITISH LITERATURE

READINGS ON

THE

HISTORIES

David L. Bender, *Publisher*

Bruno Leone, *Executive Editor*

Brenda Stalcup, *Managing Editor*

Bonnie Szumski, *Series Editor*

Clarice Swisher, *Book Editor*

Greenhaven Press, San Diego, CA

Library of Congress Cataloging-in-Publication Data

Readings on the histories of William Shakespeare / Clarice Swisher, book editor.
     p.   cm. — (The Greenhaven Press literary companion to British literature)
    Includes bibliographical references and index.
  ISBN 1-56510-556-7 (lib. bdg. : alk. paper). —
ISBN 1-56510-555-9 (pbk. : alk. paper)
  1. Shakespeare, William, 1564–1616—Histories. 2. Historical drama, English—History and criticism. 3. Great Britain—History—1066–1687—Historiography. 4. Kings and rulers in literature. 5. Middle Ages in literature. I. Swisher, Clarice, 1933– . II. Series.
PR2982.R39   1998
822.3'3—dc21   97-41139
                                                  CIP

Cover photo: The Pierpont Morgan Library, New York. PML 5122

"This blessed plot, this earth, this realm, this England, This nurse, this teeming womb of royal kings, Feared by their breed and famous by their birth."

Richard II
act 2, scene 1

CONTENTS

Chapter 2: The Richard Plays

Chapter 3: The Henry Plays

Chapter 4: The Lesser-Known History Plays

FOREWORD

"'Tis the good reader that
makes the good book."

Ralph Waldo Emerson

The story's bare facts are simple: The captain, an old and scarred seafarer, walks with a peg leg made of whale ivory. He relentlessly drives his crew to hunt the world's oceans for the great white whale that crippled him. After a long search, the ship encounters the whale and a fierce battle ensues. Finally the captain drives his harpoon into the whale, but the harpoon line catches the captain about the neck and drags him to his death.

A simple story, a straightforward plot—yet, since the 1851 publication of Herman Melville's *Moby-Dick*, readers and critics have found many meanings in the struggle between Captain Ahab and the whale. To some, the novel is a cautionary tale that depicts how Ahab's obsession with revenge leads to his insanity and death. Others believe that the whale represents the unknowable secrets of the universe and that Ahab is a tragic hero who dares to challenge fate by attempting to discover this knowledge. Perhaps Melville intended Ahab as a criticism of Americans' tendency to become involved in well-intentioned but irrational causes. Or did Melville model Ahab after himself, letting his fictional character express his anger at what he perceived as a cruel and distant god?

Although literary critics disagree over the meaning of *Moby-Dick*, readers do not need to choose one particular interpretation in order to gain an understanding of Melville's novel. Instead, by examining various analyses, they can gain numerous insights into the issues that lie under the surface of the basic plot. Studying the writings of literary critics can also aid readers in making their own assessments of *Moby-Dick* and other literary works and in developing analytical thinking skills.

The Greenhaven Literary Companion Series was created with these goals in mind. Designed for young adults, this unique anthology series provides an engaging and comprehensive introduction to literary analysis and criticism. The essays included in the Literary Companion Series are chosen for their accessibility to a young adult audience and are expertly edited in consideration of both the reading and comprehension levels of this audience. In addition, each essay is introduced by a concise summation that presents the contributing writer's main themes and insights. Every anthology in the Literary Companion Series contains a varied selection of critical essays that cover a wide time span and express diverse views. Wherever possible, primary sources are represented through excerpts from authors' notebooks, letters, and journals and through contemporary criticism.

Each title in the Literary Companion Series pays careful consideration to the historical context of the particular author or literary work. In-depth biographies and detailed chronologies reveal important aspects of authors' lives and emphasize the historical events and social milieu that influenced their writings. To facilitate further research, every anthology includes primary and secondary source bibliographies of articles and/or books selected for their suitability for young adults. These engaging features make the Greenhaven Literary Companion Series ideal for introducing students to literary analysis in the classroom or as a library resource for young adults researching the world's great authors and literature.

Exceptional in its focus on young adults, the Greenhaven Literary Companion Series strives to present literary criticism in a compelling and accessible format. Every title in the series is intended to spark readers' interest in leading American and world authors, to help them broaden their understanding of literature, and to encourage them to formulate their own analyses of the literary works that they read. It is the editors' hope that young adult readers will find these anthologies to be true companions in their study of literature.

INTRODUCTION

Each of Shakespeare's ten history plays, which collectively span more than three centuries of British history, from approximately 1200 to 1550, features a particular king. Elizabethan audiences knew this history well and recognized names and events as easily as American audiences recognize the names and events of the Revolutionary War. To the modern reader and audience, however, the histories are less familiar.

Readings on the Histories helps to clarify the figures and events of this era. The biography identifies the sources from which Shakespeare obtained his subject matter. In the appendix, a chronological list of English monarchs identifies the ten who are the subjects of Shakespeare's plays and the order in which he wrote about them. The genealogical table identifies many of the main characters of the Richard and Henry plays, who are often called both by their given names and by their titles or the houses from which they came.

The critical essays for *Readings on the Histories* are chosen to show how history is interpreted in the structure, characterization, and themes of drama. Selections represent nearly a century of criticism and include such well-known critics as Francis Fergusson, A.R. Humphreys, and E.M.W. Tillyard. The book is organized so that general topics come first, followed by separate chapters on the Richard and Henry plays and essays about the lesser-known plays.

Readings on the Histories includes many special features that make research and literary criticism accessible and understandable. An annotated table of contents lets readers quickly preview the contents of individual essays. A chronology features a list of significant events in Shakespeare's life placed in a broader historical context. The bibliography includes books on the historical periods in which the plays are set and written, on Shakespeare's life and times, and additional critical sources suitable for research.

Each essay has aids for clear understanding. The introductions serve as directed reading for the essays by explaining main points, which are then identified by subheads within the essays. Footnotes identify uncommon references and define unfamiliar words. Occasional inserts illustrate a point made in the essay or a feature of Shakespeare's play. Taken together, these aids make the Greenhaven Press Literary Companion Series an indispensable research tool.

WILLIAM SHAKESPEARE: A BIOGRAPHY

By today's standards, factual information about William Shakespeare is meager indeed; no diaries, journals, or letters survive to help biographers ascertain the author's personality, opinions, or feelings. By Elizabethan standards, however, more records exist concerning the events in Shakespeare's life than one would expect for most untitled persons. Diligent scholars have located institutional records to identify Shakespeare's place of birth and upbringing and the essential events in his family life. They have unearthed records identifying some of his employment history and economic holdings. To supplement the records, scholars have turned to the text of his works and knowledge of Elizabethan history and beliefs to understand Shakespeare the man. Not surprisingly, interpretations differ.

BIRTH AND FAMILY

William Shakespeare was born in Stratford (today called Stratford-on-Avon) in Warwickshire, a county in the heart of England, on April 23 or 24, 1564. His birth date is presumed from the record of his baptism in Holy Trinity, the Stratford Church of England, on April 26; because so many children died in infancy, baptism usually occurred within two or three days of a child's birth. Shakespeare's mother, Mary Arden, came from an old county family. More genteel and prosperous than the Shakespeares, the Ardens provided their daughter with a dowry of land and money, which advanced the status of her husband, John Shakespeare, when the couple married in 1557. John Shakespeare was a wool dealer and glove maker in Stratford and, for a time, a prominent community leader and officeholder. He began public service as the town ale taster in 1557 and subsequently performed the offices of burgess, constable, town treasurer, alderman, and bailiff, or mayor. In the early 1580s, however, John Shakespeare's financial troubles led to the loss of both his wealth and his governing positions.

William was the third of eight children born to Mary and John Shakespeare. Two daughters—Joan, christened in September 1558, and Margaret, christened in December 1662—died young. Four siblings born after William reached adulthood: Gilbert, christened in October 1566; a second Joan, christened in 1569; Richard, christened in March 1573 or 1574; and Edmund, christened in 1580. Another daughter, Anne, died when she was eight.

EDUCATION

Though no school records exist, Shakespeare likely attended public schools like the ones children throughout England attended. Typically, young children first spent a year in an elementary school for their letters (alphabet), numbers, and catechism (a book summarizing the basic principles of Christianity in question-and-answer form). After age seven, he probably attended grammar school at King's New School, where he received a rigorous education in classrooms taught by Oxford graduates—Simon Hunt and Thomas Jenkins, two of the headmasters during the years Shakespeare lived in Stratford, had advanced degrees.

Students were expected to be in their seats by six A.M. in the summer and seven A.M. in the winter for a school day that began and ended with Bible readings, psalm singing, and prayers. Students memorized Latin grammar and studied logic, Latin composition, and literature. The curriculum included the Roman dramatists Seneca, Terence, and Plautus; Renaissance religious texts; the Roman poets Horace, Virgil, and Ovid; the complete works of Dutch Renaissance scholar Erasmus; and the works of Roman orators, philosophers, and historians. Shakespeare, who drew from Ovid's *Metamorphoses* for his own plays and poems, likely remembered this classic from his grammar-school days. According to scholar and critic George R. Price, in *Reading Shakespeare's Plays*, "This education was at least comparable with a modern college major in classics." Years later, playwright Ben Jonson disparagingly called Shakespeare's learning "small Latin and less Greek," but, by Jonson's standards, "much" learning would have meant a five-year study of Latin, ending with a master's degree.

Shakespeare's education, however, extended well beyond the Stratford grammar school. Elizabethan law required regular attendance in the Protestant Church of England, so Shakespeare would have grown up listening to readings from the Bible and the *Book of Common Prayer,* the liturgical book of the Church of England. Scholars have counted in Shakespeare's plays allusions to forty books of the Bible and many references to the Ten Commandments, quotations from Psalms, and lines from the prayer book. In *Shakespeare the Man,* biographer A.L. Rowse calls Shakespeare a man educated in "the university of life." His plays display detailed knowledge of the entertainment, social mores, and culture of his native Warwickshire. Price says that we may

> be sure that the knowledge of hawking, hunting, and archery, of horses, dogs, and wild things, of peddlers, shepherds, and farm folk—this store of information in his plays and poems was not acquired only from books, but indicates a normal freedom to roam the countryside and enjoy himself.

Though he lived far from London, while a boy in Stratford Shakespeare had at least a few opportunities to experience some of its cultural riches. When John Shakespeare was bailiff, probably in 1569, troupes of players began to perform plays in the Guild Hall in Stratford. Though no records of John Shakespeare's attendance exist, as a bailiff he would surely have brought his family to the entertainments. Traveling actors continued to stage plays in Stratford every year from the time William was five years old. In 1575, Shakespeare had another taste of London life when Queen Elizabeth I visited the earl of Leicester at his castle at Kenilworth, a few miles from Stratford. Called a progress, the queen's entourage included courtiers on horseback, coaches, hundreds of servants, and numerous carts hauling supplies. Country crowds gathered to watch the procession go by and perhaps hear a word from the queen. During the queen's stay—for nearly a month—crowds surrounded the castle to watch the pageants, water shows, and fireworks displays prepared in the queen's honor.

EARLY MANHOOD

Though no record confirms this, Shakespeare left school at about age sixteen. When he was eighteen years old, he married Anne Hathaway, eight years older than he. Biographers have made much of the information that banns for the marriage were called only once, on December 1, 1582, rather than the usual three times; the inference is that church officials hurried the marriage because Anne was already pregnant. However, because Elizabethan custom considered betrothal (engagement) a binding agreement and in some instances the same as marriage, her pregnancy was less unusual than modern customs might consider it.

After the marriage, the couple lived with Shakespeare's family on Henley Street in Stratford. On May 26, 1583, their child Susanna was baptized; twenty months later the young couple had twins, baptized Hamnet and Judith on February 2, 1585. How this twenty-one-year-old man supported his family is unknown. An antiquarian and gossip, John Aubrey, born a decade after Shakespeare died, collected facts and anecdotes about public persons. In his journal, he says that someone told him that Shakespeare had taught school and worked in his father's butcher shop. Since John Shakespeare had no butcher shop, Shakespeare either worked in someone else's butcher shop or in his father's leather shop. Among the myths surrounding Shakespeare's life is the story that he was caught poaching deer in a park belonging to Sir Thomas Lucy of Charlecote, near Stratford. Historian Nicholas Rowe suggests that Shakespeare had to leave his business and family and take refuge in London to avoid prosecution, but the story has never been proved.

FIRST YEARS IN LONDON

The years 1585 to 1592 are called the "lost years" because no records of any kind document Shakespeare's movements or activities during the period. He probably went to London sometime between 1585 and 1587, possibly joining up with a company of traveling actors or striking out alone on foot. By one route, a man could walk to London in four days if he made twenty-five miles a day, lodging at inns along the way for a penny a night. In *Shakespeare: A Compact Documentary Life,* Samuel Schoenbaum describes the city Shakespeare would have found on his arrival:

> The great city of contrasts spawned stately mansions and slum tenements, gardens and midden-heaped lanes. With the Court close to hand, it was the vital nerve-center for the professions, trade, and commerce, and the arts; London nourished the English Renaissance. Only in the metropolis could a playwright of genius forge a career for himself.

When Shakespeare came to London, attending plays was the most popular form of entertainment for all classes, from poor students to aristocrats. London had several theaters: The first, built in 1576 by James Burbage, was called simply the Theatre, and the Fortune, the Swan, the Curtain, the Rose, and Blackfriars followed. The theaters were constructed with an open stage projecting into a roofless courtyard where a standing crowd viewed the performance. Three levels of covered seats surrounded the open space. Each theater had an all-male resident company of actors performing plays and competing with all the other theaters for popular approval. Female parts were played by boys usually recruited from the boys' choirs of the churches. (A woman did not act onstage until 1660.) During the twelve days of Christmas, the companies performed plays in Queen Elizabeth's court to entertain royal guests; for those performances, painted scenery identified the settings in which elaborately clad actors performed. Throughout the year, traveling troupes drawn from the companies also performed plays in towns and cities outside London.

One story goes that Shakespeare began his career by holding patrons' horses outside the theater; another says that he began as a prompter's attendant. He may have done both jobs for a short time and then advanced to acting before becoming the company's writer. Though attending plays was popular London entertainment, many moralists complained that the jokes were too bawdy and that young men neglected their church duties in favor of playgoing. Consequently, society looked on actors as riffraff at worst and men of questionable reputation at best. Price comments: "When Shakespeare became an actor, he must have deeply grieved the heart of his father and mother, and he surely gave himself cause for extreme discomfort at times." John Aubrey mentions no misgivings, however, and writes: "He was a handsome, well-shap't man: very good company, and of a very readie and pleasant smoothe Witt."

THE EMERGENCE OF A PLAYWRIGHT

Because Shakespeare was an outsider in London, a country man who lacked the sophistication and easy manners of the Cambridge and Oxford University men, he studied the ways of a gentleman, found a mentor, and read widely. Shakespeare looked to Cambridge-educated playwright Christopher Marlowe, who was the same age but who preceded Shakespeare in skillfully combining drama with poetry. In many plays throughout his career, Shakespeare pays tribute to Marlowe, though he eclipsed Marlowe as a dramatist. Shakespeare emulated the romantic elements and imitated the poetic techniques of the works of two British poets: Sir Philip Sidney's sonnets and *The Arcadia,* a prose romance, and Edmund Spenser's *The Faerie Queene,* an allegory glorifying England and Queen Elizabeth.

In addition, Shakespeare, who loved his country and her history, read the *Chronicles,* published in 1577 and reissued in 1587 by Raphael Holinshed, a historian who came to London early in Elizabeth's reign. Since there were no copyright laws in effect in the sixteenth century, writers borrowed from and paraphrased the works of other writers. Holinshed borrowed from an earlier historian, Edward Hall, whose *Chronicles* also recounted the events of England's history, especially the monarchy. Shakespeare depended on Holinshed's *Chronicles* most heavily as the source for his history plays, but he also drew on Hall and other sources. For *1, 2,* and *3 Henry VI* and *Richard III,* he selected episodes from both historians. He borrowed from Holinshed for *Richard II,* but modeled the character of his king on *The Troublesome Reign and Lamentable Death of Edward the Second* by Marlowe. Shakespeare's *King John* closely parallels an anonymous 1591 play entitled *The Troublesome Reign of John, King of England.* There is no identifiable source for Shakespeare's most popular invention, Falstaff. A Falstaff-like character had appeared as Sir John Oldcastle in a 1594 play entitled *The Famous Victories of Henry the Fifth,* from which Shakespeare borrowed and modified two incidents. Shakespeare used the name Oldcastle in the first version of *1 Henry IV,* but changed the name to Falstaff since Holinshed had written about Oldcastle, a man very different from Shakespeare's fat knight. *Henry VIII* is based on Holinshed except for incidents in the life of Archbishop of Canterbury Thomas Cranmer recorded in John Foxe's *Book of Martyrs.*

Records show that Shakespeare had already made his mark as a playwright by 1592. His early plays—*The Tragedy of Titus Andronicus; 1, 2,* and *3 Henry VI; The Comedy of Errors;* and *Richard III*—mimic the form of the Roman playwrights he studied in grammar school and three successful plays staged in the late 1580s: Thomas Kyd's *Spanish Tragedy* and Marlowe's *Tamburlaine* and *The Jew of Malta.* The three parts of *Henry VI* concern the wars in France and prepare the audience for *Richard III,* a play with one star player, the callous villain King Richard. The popularity of Shakespeare's early plays elicited a comment in a journal left by Robert Greene, a popular Cambridge-educated playwright who died in 1592. In his *Groatsworth of Wit,* Greene, complaining that the professional actors had forsaken university men like him, specifically attacked Shakespeare:

> Yes trust them not: for there is an upstart Crow, beautified with our feathers, that with his *Tygers hart wrapt in a Players hyde,*[1] supposes he is as well able to bombast out a blanke verse as the best of you: and beeing an absolute *Johannes fac totum,*[2] is in his owne conceit the onely Shake-scene in a countrey.

SHAKESPEARE AS A POET

About the time Greene's comment appeared, plague spread through London, lasting through 1593, and the lord mayor ordered the theaters closed. Without theater work, Shakespeare made his first appeal to the reading public. He had wanted to be a poet, which he considered a noble occupation; acting and writing plays, he thought, were merely means to support a family. None of his plays, which were written for live performance, had been published by 1592. On April 18, 1593, the printer Richard Field obtained license to publish Shakespeare's poem *Venus and Adonis,* and on May 9, 1594, license to publish another poem, *Lucrece.*

Shakespeare also wrote a series of 154 sonnets, which celebrate a beautiful young man and express powerful passion for a mysterious dark lady at whose hands the poet suffers greatly. Since neither the young man nor the dark lady is named, critics have gone to great lengths to try to verify their identity. Most critics conclude that the twenty sonnets dedicated to the young man and the many others that celebrate him in glowing terms refer to the earl of Southampton, who had become Shakespeare's patron. No less critical energy has also been devoted to determining whether or not the sonnets are autobiographical. Biographer A.L. Rowse, who thinks they are, agrees that the young man is the earl of Southampton and identifies the dark lady as Emilia Bassano, daughter of an Italian musician in the queen's court.

In 1594 Shakespeare turned away from sonnet writing. He also turned thirty in April of that year. With the end of the

---

1. a play on Shakespeare's line from *Henry VI,* "O tiger's heart wrapt in a woman's hide!"   2. a "John do-everything," a jack-of-all-trades

plague, the earl of Southampton's patronage ended, and with the reopening of the theaters, Shakespeare established himself with an acting company. By the summer of 1594, a group of actors formerly with other companies had formed a company under the patronage of Henry Lord Hunsdon, lord chamberlain to the queen, calling themselves Lord Chamberlain's Men. They played at various theaters including the Theatre, the Curtain, and the Swan. Among the company's permanent members were Henry Condell, John Heminge, Shakespeare, Richard Burbage (son of the Theatre's builder, James Burbage), William Sly, and Will Kempe. Burbage, the famous tragedian, and Kempe, the famous comedian, played leading roles in plays Shakespeare wrote specifically for their talents. From then on, Shakespeare was completely involved in the theater: He wrote for the company, acted in the plays, and shared in the profits. While in London, he worked hard and played little; he lived during those years as a lodger in a quiet room near the playhouse where he could write without interruption.

Shakespeare's first major successes as a playwright came between 1593 and 1598. *Love's Labour's Lost,* probably the only play without a borrowed plot, portrays current social and political life. Shakespeare's style in his early comedies shows evidence of the influence of John Lyly, who wrote eight comedies between 1580 and 1592. Adapting themes from Greek mythology, Lyly wrote in euphuistic style, an artificial style with dialogue rich in repartee and wordplay, musically turned lyrics, and elaborate imagery. Critics have called Shakespeare's early plays, such as *The Two Gentlemen from Verona,* lyrical because they contain passages of beautiful description and passionate feelings. With *A Midsummer Night's Dream,* Shakespeare had already gone beyond Lyly in inventiveness of plot and more interesting characters from the fairy world. *The Taming of the Shrew* and *The Tragedy of Romeo and Juliet* exemplify other characteristics of his early plays—intricate plots and long explanatory speeches written in stiff verse.

Besides writing comedy during this period, Shakespeare also wrote history plays about England's past kings: *Richard II, 1* and *2 Henry IV, Henry V,* and *King John.* After *Richard III,* Shakespeare realized that the War of the Roses had originated in the reign of Richard II, so the latter play is written about the earlier king. Presenting history as the personal conflict between two individuals, Richard II and Henry Boling-broke, Shakespeare introduces the belief that an individual's character determines his fate. The two parts of *Henry IV* portray the undoing of Henry IV (Henry Bolingbroke), who had wrongfully dethroned Richard, and the preparation of his son Hal to become Henry V. *King John* depicts the life of the thirteenth-century king John Plantagenet whose troublesome reign was poorly suited for a play. Moreover, G.B. Harrison notes that Shakespeare lacked a clear plan for the play's characters who alternate between human beings and symbols.

1 and *2 Henry IV* were particularly popular with audiences, who loved the humor of the knight Falstaff. Falstaff's unrestrained indulgence in sensual pleasures, his love of telling big lies, and his own laziness are offset by great good humor and consistent wit. Sidney Lee says, "Shakespeare's purely comic power culminated in Falstaff; he may be claimed as the most humorous figure in literature." When Falstaff disappeared as a character in subsequent plays, Queen Elizabeth requested that Shakespeare write another in which Falstaff falls in love. Shakespeare complied with *The Merry Wives of Windsor,* but in this play Falstaff is the butt, not the source, of humor. During this period, Shakespeare also wrote the comedies *Much Ado About Nothing* and *The Merchant of Venice,* both of which have two stories or threads of interest.

Shakespeare received praise from many sources for his early works. Among the most notable were comments by Francis Meres, a learned Cambridge graduate, who in *Palladis Tamia: Wit's Treasury* called Shakespeare the greatest man of letters.

> So the sweet witty soul of Ovid lives in mellifluous and honey-tongued Shakespeare, witness his *Venus and Adonis,* his *Lucrece,* his sugared *Sonnets* among his private friends, etc. As Plautus and Seneca are accounted the best for Comedy and Tragedy among the Latins: so Shakespeare among the English is the most excellent in both kinds for the stage.... As Epius Stolo said, that the Muses would speak with Plautus tongue if they would speak Latin: so I say that the Muses would speak with Shakespeare's fine filed phrase, if they would speak English.

Despite his growing fame, Stratford was still the center of Shakespeare's personal life, the place to which he returned each summer and in which he invested his money. In 1596 and 1597 Shakespeare was occupied with three significant family matters. First, in August 1596, Shakespeare's son Hamnet died at eleven; with his death Shakespeare lost hope of perpetuating his family's name. Anne Shakespeare was forty and could not be expected to have another child. Shakespeare expressed his grief in the play he was writing at the time, *King John:*

> Grief fills the room up of my absent child,
> Lies in his bed, walks up and down with me,
> Puts on his pretty looks, repeats his words,
> Remembers me of all his gracious parts,
> Stuffs out his vacant garments with his form.
>
> (act 3, scene 4)

Second, though he had no son to carry on the family name, Shakespeare pressed to obtain the title and coat of arms of a gentleman, a status evidently important to him. So that he could be considered born the son of a gentleman, Shakespeare applied and paid cash for a grant in the name of his father. On October 20, 1596, Garter King of Arms William Dethick issued a coat of arms with a falcon and a silver spear and declared Shakespeare a gentleman by birth. Today, the coat of arms is displayed on the Shakespeare monument at Stratford. Finally, in May 1597, Shakespeare purchased New Place, a large home in the center of Stratford with two barns and two orchards and gardens. Before he was thirty-five years old, Shakespeare had achieved the status of gentleman, property owner, and playwright, but he had lost his only male heir.

THE NEW GLOBE

In 1597, James Burbage, who had built the Theatre in 1576, died, and Lord Chamberlain's Men lost their lease. About the same time, Puritans increased their opposition to what they perceived as the immorality of the city theaters. The Lord Chamberlain's Men found backing to dismantle the Theatre, move the boards across the Thames from London's city center, and build the Globe away from the Puritans. By this time, Shakespeare had acquired enough wealth to buy a tenth share in the new theater.

The Globe outshone its competitors; it held two thousand spectators and was equipped with a bigger stage, a cellarage for graves and ghosts, a curtained space for intimate and surprise scenes, and a balcony. The audience was closer to the players, and the players had more flexibility to move quickly from scene to scene. *Henry V,* in which Shakespeare played the part of the chorus, anticipates the Globe. In the prologue, he refers to the new theater with excitement:

> A kingdom for a stage, princes to act
> And monarchs to behold the swelling scene! . . .
>   Can this cockpit[3] hold
> The vasty fields of France? Or may we cram
> Within this wooden O[4] the very casques[5]
> That did affright the air at Agincourt?[6]

In the epilogue, Shakespeare displays a characteristic humility:

> Thus far, with rough and all-unable pen,
> Our bending[7] author hath pursued the story,
> In little room[8] confining mighty men,
> Mangling by starts[9] the full course of their glory.

Though he himself may have been self-assured, he speaks as a humble gentleman throughout his works, self-deprecatingly calling himself "a worthless boat," "inferior far" to Marlowe. Others found this attitude charming, and Shakespeare soon gained a reputation for congeniality.

OUTPOURING OF COMEDIES AND TRAGEDIES

After 1598 Shakespeare's comedies and tragedies appeared quickly one after another. He turned from English history to Roman history and used the *Lives* of Greek philosopher and biographer Plutarch as a source of plots. *The Tragedy of Julius Caesar,* dated 1599, explores Brutus's character and motives. In addition, Shakespeare wrote three comedies to suit Will Kempe's comedic talents. Besides *The Merry Wives of Windsor,* Kempe starred in *As You Like It* and *Twelfth Night,* whose title comes from its performance before the queen during Twelfth Night of 1599–1600.

After 1600 Shakespeare wrote his greatest tragedies, distinguished from the earlier works by more subtle language and deeper spirit. *Hamlet* and *Othello* come first. In Shakespearean scholar and critic G.B. Harrison's view, "*Hamlet* is in every way the most interesting play ever written"; for nearly four hundred years, it has challenged actors and scholars to interpret Hamlet's character. *Othello,* a unified and focused play, portrays evil in the character of Iago as he exploits Othello's jealousy and Desdemona's innocence to destroy them and their love.

3. playhouse   4. playhouse   5. the actual helmets   6. the French village where Henry V defeated a larger French army   7. bowing   8. theater   9. marring the story by telling it in fragments

The opening of the Globe marked a new phase in Shakespeare's reputation and art. Firmly established as the leading dramatist in London, Shakespeare's art became more refined and subtle. Price says, "Art has replaced artifice. The style has become so fully expressive of the thought that audience and readers are unconscious of the poet's devices." Shakespeare, who was interested in the workings of human character, objectively displays his characters' minds in the actions and speeches he wrote for them. The soliloquies of Brutus, Hamlet, and Iago, for example, lay bare not only their intentions but their very souls.

Among his friends and fellow playwrights, Shakespeare had a reputation for writing headlong with little attention to revision. Aubrey reports playwright Ben Jonson's opinion of Shakespeare's method of writing: "He was wont to say that he never blotted out a line in his life. Sayd Ben Jonson, I wish he had blotted out a thousand." In the annual Shakespeare Lecture of the British Academy in 1972, M.M. Mahood acknowledges faults in the texts. Mahood says, "Shakespeare's plays abound in loose ends, false starts, confusions, and anomalies of every kind."

Though Shakespeare continued to write, the period from 1598 to 1604 brought significant personal diversions. In September 1601, his father died in Stratford. The following May, Shakespeare bought 107 acres of farmland in Old Stratford for £320, and in September a cottage on Walkers Street. On March 24, 1603, Queen Elizabeth, who had actively supported Lord Chamberlain's Men, died. James I succeeded her, took over the company, renamed it the King's Men, and supported the players even more avidly than the queen had, making them an official part of the court, doubling their salaries, and increasing their annual court appearances from three to thirteen. In addition, he gave them license to perform in any town or university. These changes required Shakespeare to pay greater attention to the approval of two audiences, the court and the Globe. Shakespeare's increase in income allowed him to invest £440 in tithes in parishes in Stratford and surrounding towns, investments that brought additional income of £60 a year.

THE KING'S MEN

From 1604 to 1608, as a member of the King's Men, Shakespeare's art changed again. He wrote two transitional comedies in which he experimented with techniques to work out dramatic problems. *All's Well That Ends Well*, an uneven play seldom performed, involves a young woman who tricks a man into becoming her husband. *Measure for Measure*, called a problem play because the plot poorly fits the theme, concerns a woman who compromises her chastity to save her brother.

After 1604, Shakespeare's tragedies probed even more deeply into the minds of their heroes. *The Tragedy of King Lear* was first performed in King James's court during the Christmas holidays of 1606. Critics regard *Lear* as Shakespeare's greatest play, though not his most popular. The play has a double plot; Lear suffers at the hands of his daughters and Gloucester at the hands of his son. Both die, but each has one child who remains loyal. The play's greatness lies in the psychological depth of Lear's character and the stark reality of both human nature and nature's elements.

Shakespeare wrote *Macbeth* in 1606, as a tribute to James I on the occasion of a state visit from the king of Denmark. The play is set in Scotland, James's home before he became king of England. The good character Banquo is a member of the Scottish Stuart family, ancestors of James. Shakespeare also honored the king, who was interested in witchcraft, by incorporating three witches into the play. Though he did not find King James I an honorable man, Shakespeare fulfilled his duty to the king upon whose patronage he depended. Like *Lear, Macbeth* reaches beyond the rational level into the subconscious, where primitive experiences lie in recesses of the mind; the tragic Macbeth and Lady Macbeth, having plotted the murder of King Duncan to put Macbeth on the throne, see their plot undone and suffer mental anguish before they too die.

After the four great tragedies, Shakespeare returned to Plutarch's *Lives* as a source for three more. *The Tragedy of Antony and Cleopatra* picks up Roman history where *Julius Caesar* left off. *The Tragedy of Coriolanus* is a political play in which Shakespeare exposes the weakness of all manner of politicians and presents the crowd in a tone more bitter than his exposé of the crowd in *Julius Caesar. Timon of Athens,* an unfinished play, tells about an ancient Greek mentioned briefly in Plutarch's *Lives.*

During this period, when Shakespeare wrote one or more plays a year and kept a busy schedule of productions at court and at the Globe, little is known of his personal life. His daughter Susanna married a well-known medical doctor from Stratford named John Hall on June 5, 1607. In September 1608, his mother, Mary Arden Shakespeare, died, and in October 1608, Shakespeare was named godfather to the son of Stratford alderman Henry Walker, whose son was named William in honor of Shakespeare.

In 1609 a respected publisher, Thomas Thorpe, published without Shakespeare's knowledge a book entitled *Shakespeare's Sonnets: Never Before Imprinted.* Without copyright protections, any person with a manuscript in hand could register it, publish it, and become its owner. Two factors indicate that Shakespeare had no part in the publication: The dedication appearing under the title was by the publisher, common practice when an author was not involved; and the volume contained numerous errors and even missing words, unlike the editions of the two poems that Shakespeare had prepared for printing. After Thorpe's edition, the sonnets were not reprinted until 1640; some critics think a displeased Shakespeare took measures to prevent further circulation in 1609.

THE FINAL PERIOD

After the outpouring of tragedies, Shakespeare's art changed again, in part because of changes in theater ownership and attendance. Blackfriars, a private theater owned by Richard Burbage, had been leased to a boys' company. Burbage, Shakespeare, and other actors bought back the lease and began performances there for upper-class audiences more like those at court. Blackfriars audiences liked new plays, while the public audiences at the Globe preferred old favorites. This situation suited Shakespeare, who could try new plays that were neither comedies nor tragedies at Blackfriars. Some critics have called the new plays romances; others, tragi-comedies. These plays express themes of reunion after long separation followed by reconciliation and forgiveness. The plots revolve around children lost and then found, divided parents brought together, or an innocent person threatened but saved. Before characters find a haven, they have been through storms and stress, encountered evil, or endured suffering. Rowse says: "For all their happy endings, these plays have an atmosphere full of suggestion and symbol, suffused with tears."

Shakespeare wrote four plays in this new form. *Pericles* is a transitional play, portions of which appear to have been written by a second playwright. After experimenting with *Pericles,* Shakespeare wrote *Cymbeline,* probably in 1610, a melodrama about an innocent girl who flees mistreatment and encounters a host of crises before she is reunited with her repentant husband. *The Winter's Tale,* written in 1610 or 1611, is a moving tale of wrongs committed by one generation and reconciled in the next.

The Tempest, a play written for James I to celebrate a court wedding, is Shakespeare's farewell to the theater. This fairy tale about a magician and his beautiful daughter ends with the reconciliation of two generations. G.B. Harrison praises *The Tempest:*

> Shakespeare has finally achieved complete mastery over words in the blank-verse form. This power is shown throughout the play, but particularly in some of Prospero's great speeches, . . . or in his farewell to his art. There is in these speeches a kind of organ note not hitherto heard. Shakespeare's thought was as deep as in his tragedies, but now he was able to express each thought with perfect meaning and its own proper harmony.

Prospero, the magician of *The Tempest,* recounts his tricks in words that some critics think apply aptly to Shakespeare. After cataloging the marvels he has conjured up over the years, from raging storms to corpses rising from the grave to a dimmed sun, he announces, "this rough magic / I here abjure. . . . I'll break my staff, / Bury it certain fathoms in the earth, / And . . . I'll drown my book." Shakespeare's only play after this farewell was *Henry VIII,* a series of historical episodes full of pageantry, music, and ceremony. During the June 29, 1613, performance of *Henry VIII,* a spark from a cannon set the thatch roof of the Globe alight and burned the building to the ground. Though the Globe was rebuilt by 1614, there is reason to believe that the players' books and many of Shakespeare's original manuscripts were lost in the fire.

From 1612 on, Shakespeare divided his time between Stratford and London, and once went to Parliament to lobby for better roads between the two cities. In 1612 his brother Gilbert died, followed by his brother Richard the next year. Shakespeare spent 1614 and 1615 in Stratford enjoying his retirement and his daughters, but information about his wife, Anne, seems to be nonexistent. The parish register of Holy Trinity shows that on February 10, 1616, Shakespeare's younger daughter, Judith, was married to Thomas Quiney, the son of Shakespeare's old friend Richard Quiney. On

March 25, 1616, while he was in fine health, Shakespeare
made a will. He left a dowry and additional money to Judith
and all lands and houses to his older daughter, Susanna, and
her heirs. He left his wife to the care of his daughters and
willed her the next-best bed, reasoning that Susanna and
her husband needed the bigger, better one. To his sister, he
left money for clothes and the home on Henley Street. He
gave small amounts of money to friends and money for rings
to fellow actors of the King's Men. And he left money for the
poor in Stratford. A month later, after a trip to London, he
suddenly became ill and died on April 23, 1616, at fifty-two.
As he lay dying, the chapel bell knelled for the passing of his
soul, for the man for whom love was the center of the universe and the central subject of his many works.

During his lifetime, Shakespeare made no effort to publish his works, other than the two long poems. His plays belonged to the members of the theater company, who printed
individual plays for sale when readers requested them in the
early 1600s. In 1623—the year Anne Hathaway Shakespeare
died—two actors from the King's Men, Henry Condell and
John Heminge, collected Shakespeare's plays and published
them in what is known as the First Folio, and they have been
in print ever since.

Some skeptics, doubting Shakespeare's genius and education, have speculated that his works were written by someone else. Doubts appeared as early as 1694 and recurred in
1785, when Francis Bacon was identified as a probable author. James Spedding, Bacon's editor and biographer, however, dismisses the notion. He says, "I doubt whether there
are five lines together to be found in Bacon which could be
mistaken for Shakespeare, or five lines in Shakespeare
which could be mistaken for Bacon." In 1921 Thomas
Looney theorized in *Shakespeare Identified* that Edward de
Vere, seventeenth earl of Oxford, was the true Shakespeare,
basing his research on the correspondences between de
Vere's travels, education, and social class and details in the
plays. Most reputable critics believe that such theories are
pursued by the uninformed. As Price says: "No first-rate
scholar has ever accepted the evidence offered by the Baco-
nians or others who argue that Shakespeare did not write
the dramas that his fellow-actors, Heminge and Condell,
published as his."

CHAPTER 1

Understanding Shakespeare's Histories

READINGS ON
THE HISTORIES

The Historical Background of the History Plays

Peter Saccio

Eight of Shakespeare's ten history plays focus on the fifteenth-century struggles of England's ruling Plantagenets; the other two concern the early Plantagenet king John (1199–1216) and the Tudor king Henry VIII (1509–1547). Peter Saccio summarizes the major events and identifies the key players in the Plantagenets' struggles for power in the 1400s and provides historical background for the two plays set in the earlier and later eras. Saccio taught English at Dartmouth College, authored *The Court Comedies of John Lyly,* and was a frequent contributor to the *Shakespeare Quarterly.*

Late in Shakespeare's *Richard III,* three royal ladies, the dowager queens Margaret and Elizabeth and the dowager duchess of York, sit upon the ground to catalogue their losses:

Margaret. I had an Edward, till a Richard killed him;
I had a Harry, till a Richard killed him.
[*to Elizabeth:*]
Thou hadst an Edward, till a Richard killed him;
Thou hadst a Richard, till a Richard killed him.
Duchess. [*to Margaret*].
I had a Richard too, and thou didst kill him;
I had a Rutland too, thou holpst to kill him.
Margaret. [*to Duchess*].
Thou hadst a Clarence too, and Richard killed him.
From forth the kennel of thy womb hath crept
A hellhound that doth hunt us all to death.

This passage of mingled mourning and rebuke is a fitting summary of the self-destructiveness of the royal house of

Plantagenet.[1] Margaret and the duchess, ancient enemies, lament their dead and savagely point out each other's guilt for the deaths. But *who* are all these people? Some the play-goer or play-reader knows: the murderous Richard is the hero-villain of the piece, and several scenes have been devoted to his killing Clarence and the Edward and Richard of lines three and four. But Harry has appeared in this play only as a corpse, while the Edward of line one and the duchess's Richard and Rutland perished in an earlier play much less familiar to modern audiences. All these persons, moreover, are not only intricately related to each other in a prolific royal house, but also surrounded by a gallery of Norfolks, Suffolks, Warwicks, and Northumberlands[2] connected to them by blood, marriage, alliance, or common interests, a throng confusing to a modern reader who tries to keep track of the large casts.

SHAKESPEARE'S TEN HISTORY PLAYS

Shakespeare wrote eight plays on the later Plantagenets. Oddly, he did not write them in chronological order. He started with a tetralogy on the events from 1422 to 1485—the three parts of *Henry VI, Richard III*—and then, dovetailing into the previous work, composed a tetralogy whose story runs from 1398 to 1422—*Richard II,* the two parts of *Henry IV, Henry V.* Although the plays vary in quality, the first set being prentice work compared to the second, and although the reverse-chronological order of writing suggests that he started with an incomplete vision of the whole, the series of eight has high coherence as a history of fifteenth-century England. Indeed, far more than any professional historian, and despite the fact that the professionals have improved upon him in historical accuracy, Shakespeare is responsible for whatever notions most of us possess about the period and its political leaders. It is he who has etched upon the common memory the graceful fecklessness of Richard II, the exuberant heroism of Henry V, the dazzling villainy of Richard III. . . .

Aside from the double tetralogy, Shakespeare wrote two other plays on English history, one on King John (reigned 1199–1216) and one on Henry VIII (reigned 1509–1547).

1. family name of the line of English kings from Henry II to Richard III (1154–1485)
2. counties in England. Dukes and earls are frequently called by the names of their counties in place of their given names

These are also fairly intricate works, and about these kings as well Shakespeare could expect at least some of his audience to be knowledgeable. Since both of these plays are entirely self-contained works, not part of a series employing cross-reference between plays, their potential for confusing the reader is somewhat smaller. They present a different version of the problem: moderns are surprised by the contents of the plays. Nowadays if ordinary readers know anything at all about John before they take up the play, they know that his barons forced him to seal Magna Carta,[3] an event that is held to be of great constitutional significance in the history of English-speaking peoples. Shakespeare does not even allude to Magna Carta, although the play dramatizes the baronial revolt that led to it. If ordinary readers know anything about Henry VIII, they know that he married six wives and brought about the English Reformation.[4] There may also leap to mind the image of a cruel and gross king, handy with the chopping block and boorish in his table manners. Shakespeare's play, however, includes only two of the wives, deals scantily with the Reformation, and generally portrays the king with the greatest respect. With these two kings, Shakespeare has had little influence upon the common memory. Constitutional struggles after Shakespeare's time endowed Magna Carta with its present nearly sacred character, and the popular notion of Henry VIII owes a great deal to Holbein's[5] paintings, a television series, movies, and historical romances. . . .

STRUGGLES IN THE ROYAL HOUSE OF PLANTAGENET

Since Shakespeare's version [of the fifteenth century] is dominated by a struggle within the royal house, the following summary stresses the dynastic issue. We must begin with Edward III, seventh of the Plantagenet kings and ruler of England for the middle half of the fourteenth century (1327–1377). This monarch's extraordinary capacity for begetting offspring lies at the root of subsequent internecine strife. Of his twelve legitimate children, five sons grew up, were endowed with extensive powers and possessions within the kingdom, and passed these on to their issue. As long as the royal family itself remained united, Edward's generosity to

3. the charter of English political and civil liberties granted by King John at Runnymede in June 1215   4. establishment of the Protestant Church   5. Hans Holbein the Younger was a German-born artist known for his portraits

his sons constituted an effective policy for governing England. In the absence of family harmony, the kingdom was almost sure to follow the Plantagenets into disorder.

Family harmony hinged largely upon the strength of the king. Unfortunately, Edward III's eldest son and heir, Edward the Black Prince, predeceased his father. Consequently, upon Edward III's death the crown went to a boy ten years old, the Black Prince's son Richard II. Although Richard stayed on the throne for twenty-two years, distinguishing himself in several crises by great personal courage, his reign never fully recovered from the circumstances of its inception. Surrounded as he was by powerful, not to say greedy, uncles and cousins, Richard the child was perforce submissive and Richard the adult tyrannically vengeful. Finally, in 1399, he overreached himself. After the death of his most powerful uncle, John of Gaunt, duke of Lancaster, he seized the Lancastrian estates. Gaunt's son Henry of Bolingbroke, exiled in Paris, returned to England and gathered an army. Although Bolingbroke's professed aim was merely the recovery of his inheritance, he soon pushed Richard off the throne, into prison, and (some months later) into his grave, there being little else to do with a deposed medieval king.

As Henry IV, first king of the Lancaster branch, Bolingbroke was a ruler with obvious liabilities: a flawed title to his crown, blood on his hands, and debts in his pocket. Of the three, the debts were the most immediately important. Various noblemen had helped him to his precarious height. As soon as he displeased them (and no king can afford continual complaisance), it occurred to them to help him down again. For most of his reign, Henry's energies were consumed in meeting rebellions. As he was a shrewd politician and a competent soldier, he contrived to defeat the dissidents and die in his bed (1413). The record of his son was more spectacular. Henry V was another shrewd politician and probably the best general ever to sit on the English throne. Reviving an old claim of the English kings to the crown of France, he united his nobles by leading an expeditionary army across the Channel. At the end of two campaigns he was the acknowledged master of both kingdoms.

At this climactic moment history began to repeat itself. In 1422 Henry V died of dysentery at the age of thirty-five. The heir to two crowns, his son Henry VI, was nine months old. The house of Lancaster, having won its throne out of the turmoils of a royal minority, came to grief two generations later by producing a similar vacuum at the center of power.

Henry VI remained king of England for nearly forty years, but only nominally. The royal child became an adult saintly in personal character, incompetent in politics, and subject to occasional mental derangement. The royal uncles and cousins, in concert and in rivalry, asserted themselves. Driven out of France, which had been reinvigorated by Joan of Arc, they retired to England to bicker with each other. By the 1450s, their quarrelling had become armed conflict. In 1460, one of the royal cousins went so far as to claim superior right to Henry's crown. This was Richard, duke of York, descended on both sides from sons of Edward III. Since his mother was heiress of the Mortimer family, the line springing from John of Gaunt's elder brother Lionel, Richard did indeed have a powerful claim, although it depended upon the principle that the royal succession could pass through a female—a controversial notion. The civil war thereupon became the dynastic struggle conventionally known as the Wars of the Roses: the Yorkists (white rose), led by Richard, versus the Lancastrians (red rose), led nominally by Henry but actually by his remarkable wife, the energetic Margaret of Anjou. When the dust finally settled, Richard, Henry, and Henry's son Edward were all dead, and occupying the throne was the house of York in the person of Richard's eldest son, Edward IV.

Except for a brief Lancastrian restoration in 1470–1471, Edward ruled competently for twenty-two years. Indeed, according to the arguments of recent historians, the reorganization of government that created the strong monarchy of the next century was in good part Edward's work. Dynastically, however, he created two serious difficulties for his house. First, instead of marrying the usual foreign princess, he wed an English widow named Elizabeth Woodville, a lady with an extraordinary quantity of relatives who promptly took advantage of their new royal connection by securing for themselves an abundance of titles, posts, and wealthy spouses. The inevitable quarrels between the older nobility and the upstart Woodvilles boded ill for the house of York. All might have been well but for the other dynastic difficulty: Edward died at the age of forty, when his two sons, Edward V and Richard, were but twelve and nine years old.

The familiar script was acted out once more, but this time

at top speed. When Edward died in April 1483, the Wood-villes had custody of the young princes, whereas by the king's will authority was to reside in his brother Richard, duke of Gloucester, who had no use at all for Woodvilles. Within three months and without a battle, the Woodvilles were out, the princes had disappeared forever, and Glouces-ter was crowned Richard III.

HENRY TUDOR ENDS THE PLANTAGENET DYNASTY

Richard's bold stroke, however, gave him only a two-year reign. In August 1485, one Henry Tudor invaded England from France, and the treachery of some of Richard's follow-ers cost the last Plantagenet king his life at the battle of Bosworth. Henry claimed the crown by right of conquest and by Lancastrian inheritance: his mother was descended from the Beaufort family, John of Gaunt's bastard offspring who had been legitimated when Gaunt made his mistress his third wife. This rather feeble dynastic claim was strength-ened by parliamentary confirmation and by Henry's subse-quent marriage to Elizabeth of York, eldest daughter to Ed-ward IV and sister to the missing princes. York and Lancaster were united in the new house of Tudor. The claim was made impregnable by Henry's efficiency as a king and by his and his son Henry VIII's thoroughness in disposing of the re-maining Plantagenet heirs. The dynastic quarrel was over.

The preceding summary of fifteenth-century English his-tory makes the dynastic issue paramount. Royal persons argue over who has the right to the crown; laws of inheri-tance and precise family relationships appear to control events altogether. To rest there, however, would be to falsify the picture. For example, given female succession, Richard, duke of York, did have a better claim than his cousin Henry VI. He refrained, however, from pressing that claim for many years; even after he asserted it, he was content at one point to be declared Henry's heir rather than his replacement. The original usurpation, that of Henry IV in 1399, was accom-plished without much thought being given to the superior rights of the Mortimer line that was later to prove so trou-blesome. There was in the fifteenth century no written law governing inheritance of the crown, not even any estab-lished practice beyond the first principle that the eldest son of a king should succeed. Even the case of a grandson, as with Richard II, could raise some question, let alone circumstances involving more than two generations or descent through a woman. The various acts of parliament confirming monarchical titles in this period did little more than ratify accomplished fact, producing the genealogical justification appropriate to the case at hand and conveniently omitting whatever else might be said about the family tree. Whether parliament even had the right to declare who was king was a very delicate matter, debated then, and still under discussion by constitutional historians. This does not mean that anybody with sufficient influence, military capacity, and luck could have secured the crown for himself. The blood royal was necessary. Henry Tudor's promise to join his Lancastrian claim to the Yorkist claim by marrying a Yorkist princess brought him significant support. Given *some* dynastic justification, however, other factors determined the outcome.

NONFAMILY INFLUENCES ON POWER

Of other factors there was an abundance. International politics played a role. Edward IV's recovery from the brief Lancastrian restoration of 1470–1471 was made possible by the assistance of the duke of Burgundy. Henry Tudor's attack on Richard III received aid from the king of France. Needless to say, these continental rulers were not acting out of disinterested charity. England, France, and Burgundy were engaged in ceaseless diplomatic maneuvering, each power fearful of alliance between the other two.

Probably more important than external pressures were social and economic conditions within England. The original Lancastrian usurpation was for many people vindicated by the success of the first two Lancastrian kings. Only in the social chaos of Henry VI's time, when the incompetence and the injustice of Henry's government were exacerbated by chagrin at the loss of France, did the York-Mortimer claim receive significant support. Edward IV's hold on the crown was in turn made acceptable to most people by his strenuous effort to correct local abuses and stabilize the royal finances. The usurpation of his brother Richard III was welcomed by some who feared another prolonged royal minority and who respected Richard as an energetic administrator.

Possibly even more important influences upon events—at least at any given moment—were the ambitions of individual noblemen outside the royal family. The immediate success of a royal claimant depended very largely upon his ability to attract support from nobles who could call up a fighting force, and these nobles were not driven by abstract passions for the rights of Lancaster or York. They aimed to secure properties or protect rights of their own; an alliance with a Henry or an Edward arose from temporarily congruent interests. Much betrayal and side-switching resulted. In 1455–1461, for example, the house of York had no greater ally than the earl of Warwick, who was the duchess of York's nephew; yet in 1470 Warwick betrothed his daughter to the Lancastrian heir and drove Edward IV temporarily from the throne. Perhaps influenced by modern civil wars fought on fundamental ideological issues, we are likely to imagine the York-Lancaster strife as an affair of more massive, coherent, and irreconcilable parties than was the case. Our inclination is reinforced by the romantic label, the Wars of the Roses, evoking as it does a vision of England divided into two camps whose members proudly flourished their red or white badges. In fact, there was almost no ideology involved, the armies were very small, and England went unscathed by any general destruction of life or property. As for the roses, they were made prominent by the Tudor historians rather than the Plantagenet combatants, popularized by Shakespeare, and turned into the standard formal name for the war only in the nineteenth century.[6]

BIASED VIEWS OF FIFTEENTH-CENTURY HISTORY

Just what did happen in the fifteenth century remains in many respects a puzzle. Vital documentary evidence has survived incompletely. Contemporary accounts are few in number, written by less talented chroniclers than those of the earlier Middle Ages, infected by rumor, and occasionally disfigured by prejudice in favor of one king or another. Modern historians have treated the period as something of a stepchild, a disorderly interlude between the achievements of the early Plantagenets and those of the Tudor Renaissance. . . .

There is a modern understanding of what happened in the

---

6. As S.B. Chrimes has pointed out, the Plantagenets had many heraldic badges. A red rose was only one of those used by the dukes of Lancaster and their descendants Henry IV and Henry V, and it was not employed by Henry VI, the Lancastrian king under whom the wars were fought. Richard, duke of York, inherited a white rose from the Mortimers, but it was seldom used by Edward IV and never by Richard III. Henry VII revived the Lancastrian red rose and, to emphasize his union of the rival houses, invented the Tudor double rose, white superimposed upon red.

fifteenth century, incomplete and full of questions though it
be, built up by research historians. Secondly, there is a Tudor
understanding. Henry VII commissioned an Italian human-
ist, Polydore Vergil, to write an official history of England.
Vergil's book is the foundation of a lively tradition of Tudor
historiography, culminating in two works that were Shakespeare's principal sources of information: Edward Hall's *The
Union of the Two Noble and Illustre Families of Lancaster
and York* (1548) and Raphael Holinshed's *The Chronicles of
England, Ireland, and Scotland* (1578; Shakespeare used the
second edition, 1587). Basic to these Tudor accounts is a belief in Henry VII as the savior of England. In part this belief
sprang from the necessity to justify the Tudor acquisition of
the throne: Richard III, for example, is made more spectac-
ularly villainous than any man could possibly be, so that
Tudor monarchy may appear the more desirable. In part the
belief arose from the widespread sixteenth-century conviction that secular history displays patterns reflecting God's
providential guidance of human affairs. Thus the deposition
of Richard II is seen as a sacrilegious act interrupting the
succession of God's anointed kings, a kind of original sin for
which England and her rulers must suffer. The Lancastrians
are then punished for their usurpation by the Yorkists, and
the Yorkists by their own last king, until, England having
atoned in blood, redemption may come in the form of Henry
Tudor and his union of the rival houses. Thirdly, there is a
Shakespearean perspective. This is, of course, still largely
Tudor, since Shakespeare is writing during the reign of
Henry's granddaughter, Queen Elizabeth, and drawing his
material from Hall and Holinshed. Nonetheless, despite their
large areas of agreement, the Tudor chroniclers, poets, and
playwrights who dealt with historical matters (there were
many) were certainly capable of individual interpretations of
men and events. Shakespeare especially deviates from the
received accounts because he is translating relatively form-
less chronicles into drama, taking historical liberties out of
artistic necessity. Although there are limits on the liberties
he can take—there is no point at all in writing a history play
about Richard III if you have him *win* at Bosworth—he can,
and does, change the personalities of historical figures, in-
vent characters, compress the chronology, alter the geogra-
phy, devise confrontations that never took place, commit
anachronisms, and so forth. Margaret of Anjou, whose sav-

age lamentations were quoted at the beginning of this view-point had in fact been dead for a year at the time the scene is supposed to occur. Above all, Shakespeare personalizes. Whether or not history is really governed by the characters and the choices of individual men and women, the dramatist can only write as if it were. Social conditions, cultural habits, economic forces, justice and the lack of it, all that we mean by "the times," must be translated into persons and passions if they are to hold the stage.

What Are Shakespeare's Histories?

Lily B. Campbell

Lily B. Campbell reviews critics who have defined or described Shakespeare's histories and variously distinguished them from his other plays as patriotic expressions, political pieces, artistic dramatizations of past events and personages, and serious plays about state events and public morality. Lily B. Campbell, who has taught at the University of California in Los Angeles, is the author of *Scenes and Machines on the English Stage* and *Shakespeare's Tragic Heroes: Stories of Passion.*

When Shakespeare's editors arranged his plays in the First Folio, they grouped them into Comedies, Histories, and Tragedies, putting the ten plays dealing with English history, and only those, into the *Histories* classification. The why of this arrangement implies definition. What was a history play in the thinking of the editors? Many scholars have discussed the genre without having agreed upon a definition.

Clearly the editors of the First Folio did not accept the authority of the titles of such plays as had already appeared in quarto editions [which called some histories "tragedies" and some comedies and tragedies "histories"]. . . .

Clearly, also, the editors did not differentiate histories from tragedies on the basis of the sources from which they were derived, for the plays listed as histories have their source in the same chronicles as *Lear* and *Macbeth* among the tragedies, and *Cymbeline* among the comedies. Most of the Shakespeare tragedies were, indeed, drawn from accepted historical sources. What, then, differentiated the chosen ten in the thinking of Shakespeare's first editors?

The answer to these questions is usually vague. Many scholars have substituted description for definition in writ-

From *Shakespeare's "Histories": Mirrors of Elizabethan Policy*, by Lily B. Campbell (San Marino, CA: Huntington Library, 1947). Reprinted with the permission of the Henry E. Huntington Library.

ing about Shakespeare's histories. [In *Literary Remains*, Samuel Taylor] Coleridge, seeing that the ten plays related to the history of England, and taking into account his premise that the history play should be regarded as "the transitional link between the epic poem and the drama," framed a definition to fit the facts as he saw them:

> In order that a drama may be properly historical, it is necessary that it should be the history of the people to whom it is addressed.... It takes, therefore, that part of real history which is least known, and infuses a principle of life and organization into the naked facts, and makes them all the framework of an animated whole.

It is difficult to see why Coleridge should regard plays dealing with the Wars of the Roses as "least known" to the Elizabethans, for this period was the one most frequently chronicled and made the subject of exegesis by the Tudors. But it is quite easy to see why he arrived at his definition of a true history as dealing with the people to whom it is addressed, since that apparently seemed to him the only basis upon which the ten English histories could have been differentiated from many of the others. It is evident, however, that he saw the inadequacy of his own definition, for he recognized the existence of varied types of history plays, calling *Henry IV*, for instance, a "mixed drama" and explaining:

> The distinction does not depend on the mere quantity of historical events in the play compared with the fictions; for there is as much history in "Macbeth" as in "Richard," but in the relation of the history to the plot. In the purely historical plays, the history forms the plot: in the mixed, it directs it; in the rest, as Macbeth, Hamlet, Cymbeline, Lear, it subserves it.

The purpose of the history play Coleridge saw as familiarizing the people of a country with the great names from their past and thereby arousing "a steady patriotism, a love of just liberty, and a respect for all those fundamental institutions of social life, which bind men together."

ELIZABETHANS TAKE PRIDE IN THEIR HISTORY

Professor Schelling in his book on *The English Chronicle Play*, published in 1902, made probably the most effective contribution thus far to the recognition of the importance of the genre and to the history of its development. He alone recognized that the history play was more closely affiliated with historical literature than with other varieties of the drama. But he found its roots in the tide of patriotism which swept England at the time of the threat from the Spanish Armada,[1] and he saw it withering with the "un-English prince," King James of Scotland, on the throne of England.[2] Professor Schelling would recognize two groups of history plays: those centering about history and historical personages, and those dealing with legendary history, or at least involving a more or less conscious deviation from history.

Professor Tucker Brooke in his small volume on *The Tudor Drama,* published in 1911, devoted a chapter to the history play which has been the basis for a good deal of the teaching of the subject to college students. He isolated two main causes as accounting for the popularity of the history play during the last years of Elizabeth: "an unusual public interest in the matters treated in such plays; and particular stage conditions which ... greatly stimulated the demand for dramas constructed on the loose and facile pattern usual to this type." Professor Brooke recognized the great interest of the Elizabethans in the history of foreign lands as well as their own, but he did not analyze the nature of the "matters treated in such plays" which interested them. Inevitably, like his predecessors, he found difficulty in defining the history play and chose to describe its various forms rather than to confine it in any formula. He listed plays of mixed type, biographical plays, histories of tragic type, romanticized treatments of history, and a most important group which he described as

> Plays *par excellence* of national feeling or national philosophy, where the normal interest in *dramatis personae* is more or less absorbed either in the expression of patriotic sentiment or in the interpretation of problems of government and statecraft. It is this class which gives to the Elizabethan history play its individuality as a dramatic species.

The many noble utterances of patriotic fervor which occur in Shakespeare's histories have led most students to think of the plays as patriotic plays, and the fact that the most notable of the plays were produced in the ten or twelve years immediately following the defeat of the Armada has led to the very common acceptance of a *post hoc, ergo propter hoc*[3] explanation. But the descriptions of the history play as essentially the expression of the great patriotic ardor which centered about the victory of 1588, as resulting from the "tri-

1. a fleet of Spanish warships defeated by British warships in the English Channel in 1588   2. as James I, ruling from 1603 to 1625   3. after this, therefore because of this

umphant exhilaration" of the Armada year, as exhibiting "exuberant nationalism," and as being "jubilant in pride of country and of race," ignore, strangely enough, the fact that with the exception of *Henry V* and perhaps *Henry VIII,* Shakespeare's plays were written, not about the admirable rulers of England and their times, but rather about those rulers who had sowed the wind and reaped the whirlwind. We should hardly expect that in the United States a great spirit of exuberant nationalism, a proud jubilation in victory, would result in plays centering about Presidents Buchanan and Harding. It seems just as unlikely that the desire to celebrate the greatness of England should result in plays about Richard II, who was deposed for his sins; or Henry IV and his rebel-ridden kingdom; or Richard III, infamous for his tyranny; or Henry VI, who "lost France, and made his England bleed." Surely, the implied definition of patriotism, limiting it to its prideful and jubilant aspects, is too narrow to cover Shakespeare's loyal but searching study of England's past.

THE HISTORIES AS POLITICAL PLAYS

August Wilhelm Schlegel long ago provided a key to the meaning of the Shakespeare histories when he said [in *Lectures on Dramatic Art and Literature*] that they, as a series, furnish "examples of the political course of the world, applicable to all times," though he did not use his key to unlock the specific significance of the individual plays in relation to the times in which they were written.

When in 1929 Professor H.B. Charlton published his lecture on *Shakespeare, Politics, and Politicians,* he went further with the statement that a better name for the history plays would be political plays, "for they are plays in which the prevailing dramatic interest is in the fate of a nation." Very disappointingly he then defined the political purpose of the plays as "exercising and fostering patriotism" and gave the old description of the England of the Armada. . . .

However, Professor Charlton did face squarely the dilemma of patriotic plays written about the nation's rulers who are least to be emulated:

> But what ultimately will distinguish the history-play from tragedy is beginning to appear. Comedy and tragedy are concerned with the eternal or ephemeral fate of individual men. The history play is concerned with communities of men, and

primarily with nations. The real hero of the English play is England.

Having taken the important step of recognizing the plays as political, and having defined the interest in history as an interest in nations, he was thus led to a conclusion which seems to me utterly without justification, that England is the hero of the plays. Accepting England as the hero but fully aware of the far from noble conduct of the English heroes who act for the hero England, he was forced to the decision that national politics are to be judged on general Machiavellian principles,[4] for even in *Henry V* there is

> the sense that not only is politics a nasty business, but that a repugnant unscrupulousness is an invaluable asset in the art of government. That is the burden of the English History Plays, jubilant as they are in pride of country and of race.

J.A.R. Marriott anticipated Professor Charlton in considering the plays as political plays in his *English History in Shakespeare* and in his more important paper on "Shakespeare and Politics," where he examined the plays to find what was said

> upon "Politics" as properly understood: upon the science of government and the art of statesmanship; upon man's place in the πολις; upon the reciprocal obligations of ruler and ruled; upon the relation of the citizen and the commonwealth.

It is in distinguishing between Shakespeare's continually derogatory references to *politicians* and his constant concern with *politics* in the true meaning of the word that Marriott made his most significant contribution, but he went further than this in stating certain premises necessary to the understanding of Shakespeare's history plays. First, he stressed what no critic should ever forget—that Shakespeare was above all a playwright, "possessed of pre-eminent skill in delineation of character by means of dialogue," and that we must be wary of "identifying Shakespeare's sentiments with those of his puppets." Second, he insisted that Shakespeare's approach to contemporary problems in politics or religion was an indirect approach, for he was too great an artist "to allow contemporary problems in politics or religion to obtrude themselves directly into his drama," and that if he wanted to teach the ecclesiastical controversies of the

4. the idea that the end justifies the means

time, he would do it not by reference to the "Jesuit mission" but by picturing the relations between King John and Pope Innocent III. Third, he said, Shakespeare as a dramatist was of necessity only incidentally a philosopher, politician, or historian. Finally, he reaffirmed the "law of the universal" as the law to which Shakespeare like every great artist must conform, so that his appeal may always be to humanity at large and not merely to any one nation.

Having oriented the discussion by his definition of politics and his premises as to Shakespeare the artist, Marriott concluded that the theme of Shakespeare's history plays is the evil of civil dissension, domestic discord, and unnatural controversy as set forth by Edward Halle in the first sentence of his chronicle, that he pictures in *King John* the peril to the State of internal divisions, in *Richard II* the political amateur, in *Henry IV* the professional politician, in *Henry V* saintly strength, and in *Henry VI* saintly weakness. In the plays concerning the Wars of the Roses, "Shakespeare, with unerring dramatic instinct, turned aside from political philosophy and seized upon the personal aspects of the disorders of that day."

But because the premises are in general so eminently sound and so universally held, it does not follow that the conclusions are equally acceptable. It seems necessary, then, to detour from the matter of definition to discuss them briefly. That Shakespeare was first of all a playwright and skillful in the portrayal of character by dialogue, and that his characters did not necessarily utter the author's sentiments, is a statement to which with most other critics I can but say "Amen." But a dramatist is more than a portrayer of character by dialogue. His most important business is with plot, if we agree with Aristotle that his drama is or should be the representation of an action. In his interpretation of the individual plays Marriott has indicated that Shakespeare "turned aside from political philosophy and seized upon the personal aspects of the disorders of that day," a logical result of this omission of plot from the business of the dramatist. Perhaps Richard II does appear as an amateur politician, but it does not follow that the play of *Richard II* is a play concerned with amateur politics. Our concern should be to ask what the plot says.

That Shakespeare's approach to any contemporary problem of politics or religion must, because he was an artist, have been an indirect approach cannot be disputed if taken to mean only that Shakespeare did not use his plays as polemical tracts. But the use of the word *indirect* ignores the fact that . . . the chief function of history was considered to be that of acting as a political mirror. The idea of holding the mirror up to nature (or to politics) pervaded the whole conception of art during the Elizabethan period, but to identify the conception of the mirror with indirection seems to me inaccurate.

THE HISTORIES AS STATE EVENTS AND PUBLIC MORALITY

That Shakespeare as a dramatist was only incidentally philosopher, politician, or historian is a contention that takes us back almost to the question of whether the egg or the hen comes first, but it is a fundamental question in the criticism of all the arts, reminiscent as it is of the theory of "art for art's sake." Marriott quoted the wise words of Sir Walter Raleigh (the second) reminding us that Shakespeare "had a meaning even while Drama was his trade," though I would suggest that *medium* is a better word than *trade*, for if we are considering Shakespeare as an artist rather than a craftsman, it is more fitting to consider the creator or interpreter of life in relation to his medium of expression. Certainly Shakespeare did not, so far as we know, write a treatise on moral philosophy or a political discourse or a history of England. His medium was the drama, and through the drama he said what he had to say. His medium made concrete what another man might say of philosophy or political theory in a treatise dealing with abstractions or generalizations. He represented an action with its causes and its results, so that it had a beginning, a middle, and an end. The action was put into being by concrete and specific persons on the stage; as living beings they spoke and did their deeds of good or evil, and as living persons they hated and loved and feared and rejoiced. But because Shakespeare used the medium of the drama to express what he had to say, there is no reason for denying to him a moral and a political philosophy which motivated first the choice of story and second the plotting of that story.

To return, then, after this detour, to the main question: What is a history play? The Elizabethans expected any work of history to act as a political mirror, to be concerned with *politics* in the sense in which Marriott defined the term. And a history play must be regarded as a literary medium for history. If it is understood that a history play is concerned with politics, furthermore, the point of its divergence from tragedy becomes clear, for the divisions of philosophy known as *ethics* and *politics* were familiar from the very titles of Aristotle's works and represented the accepted approaches to the study of human conduct. For instance, the popular orations of the much revered Isocrates, translated into English as *A Perfite Looking Glass for All Estates,* opened with an "Oration of Morall Instructions . . . : contayning a perfite description of the duetye of every private person," which was followed by an "Oration of Morall Instructions as Touching the Dutie of Princes and Magistrates and the Well Governing of a Commonweale." Spenser, writing the great Tudor epic, proposed to organize his poem about this dual concept, and he pointed out the fact that he was following the examples of Homer and Virgil and Ariosto and Tasso in so doing. He called the divisions of philosophy *Ethice* and *Politice,* the one concerned with the private moral virtues, the other with the public or political virtues. What Professor W.D. Ross said of Aristotle could be equally well said of Shakespeare:

> he does not forget in the *Ethics* that the individual man is essentially a member of society, nor in the *Politics* that the good life of the state exists only in the good lives of its citizens.

Nevertheless, the dividing line is there, and it is to this distinction between private and public morals that we must look for the distinction between tragedy and history. Tragedy is concerned with the doings of men which in philosophy are discussed under *ethics;* history with the doings of men which in philosophy are discussed under *politics.*

The Family in Shakespeare's Histories

Robert B. Pierce

Robert B. Pierce explores Shakespeare's treatment of the family in the ten history plays. In the first four— *1, 2,* and *3 Henry VI* and *Richard III*—Shakespeare makes the family a symbolic microcosm of the state; disorder and treachery within families mirror the forces that can topple a kingdom. Pierce identifies *King John* and *Richard II* as experimental plays and describes how the two parts of *Henry IV* and *Henry V* bring the themes of family and state together because they concern the effects of public roles on the private man. Robert B. Pierce, who has done extensive research into the themes of the history plays, has contributed numerous articles to scholarly journals.

The family is so basic a human institution that in almost any play or group of plays it has an important role. Shakespeare's history plays are primarily concerned with the public life of his nation, the terrible hundred years of civil strife and wars against the French that haunted the imagination of Elizabethan England and that earlier time of crisis in the reign of King John. His plays express the deepest and most widespread feelings of his countrymen. To them political matters were not of merely theoretical concern; they dreaded the return of a chaos that they knew would involve them and their families in untold suffering. In our age we have trouble responding to or even understanding the *eros* that Elizabethans felt toward their autocratic queen. The principles of order and succession are abstractions, but in the Elizabethans they evoked the most intensely personal feeling.

No man could avoid showing the family in history plays since kings and princes are necessarily fathers and sons, husbands and brothers. But Shakespeare's special contribu-

From *Shakespeare's History Plays: The Family and the State,* by Robert B. Pierce (Columbus: Ohio State University Press, 1971). Reprinted by permission of the author.

tion is to make the language and episodes of family life relevant to the political themes of the plays. In a kind of drama shaped by Tudor[1] political ideas, Shakespeare makes the family a microcosm of the state and an echo of its values. Marriage and the relationship of father and son, brother and brother, the noble and his house—these are the stuff of a personal drama. He relies on them to give immediacy to his panoramic views of the rise and fall of kings and kingdoms. Ready to his hand is a tradition of seeing in the family a symbol of the state, part of the Elizabethan habit of finding correspondences among all levels of existence. Hence there are traces of the family used similarly in other history plays of the period as well as in the chronicles, moral tracts, and even official pronouncements like the Homilies. But Shakespeare goes beyond his fellows by turning this use of the family into a formal principle, an important part of the whole structure of the plays.

LANGUAGE AND MIRROR-SCENES EMPHASIZE FAMILY THEMES

His most conventional use of the family is in the images of family life that permeate the language of the plays. For all the growth of his poetic technique during the 1590s, in *Henry V* he is still inclined to make his references to family relationships abstract and rhetorical. The power of such utterances can be great. Henry V evokes the brutality of war with remarkable clarity when he warns the citizens of Harfleur of the violence facing them, the rape of their daughters and the murder of their infants and aged fathers. But neither the abstract content nor the formal syntax of such passages has changed greatly since Bedford's grotesque description in *1 Henry VI* of the chaos to follow Henry V's death:

> When at their mothers' moist eyes babes shall suck,
> Our isle be made a nourish of salt tears,
> And none but women left to wail the dead.

> (I.i.49–51)

All the plays are full of generalized references to the doctrine of moral inheritance, to loyalty and order in the family, and to the impact of political order and disorder on the family. At their best these can be striking, and their frequency gives them cumulative effect over the whole span of history plays.

---

1. the family name of English monarchs who ruled from 1485–1603: Henry VII, Henry VIII, Edward VI, Mary I, and Elizabeth I

Most important, they provide an undercurrent that complements more extensive uses of the family.

Closely related to this poetic technique is the emblematic[2] episode or mirror-scene. In it one of the stock images, such as a father and son's estrangement through political strife, is given fuller dramatic expression in a brief action more or less detachable from the plot of the play. These scenes are simplest and most obvious in the early plays. Henry VI looks on at the battle of Towton in *3 Henry VI* while a father discovers that he has killed his son and a son that he has killed his father. Here a weak monarch watches helplessly as the horrors of civil disorder pass from public to private life. Though the first tetralogy[3] is full of such effects, Shakespeare may have grown tired of their comparative simplicity. In *Richard II* he dissipates the emblematic significance of York's denunciation of his treacherous son by tinging the scenes with savage comedy.

In the later plays such episodes are more a part of their dramatic context and less marked by a heightened, artificial style. Much less formal than the emblematic scenes of the Henry VI plays are those in *1 Henry IV* in which the domestic happiness of the conspirators, especially Hotspur and his wife, provides ironic contrast with the national upheaval they are bringing about. The effect is all the richer for being less conspicuous, more appropriate to the overall tone and dramatic structure.

But these uses of the family are essentially figurative; they are not part of the central dramatic action as it expresses the characters and fates of the main agents in the historical narrative. Acting or refusing to act, men produce historical events, and the character that governs their political behavior reveals itself as well in their domestic lives. One frequent pattern of these plays is that the man and the statesman overlap, that virtues in the one are virtues in the other. Henry VI fails as king and husband; Henry V is victorious at Agincourt and in wooing Katherine.

PARALLEL PATTERNS IN PUBLIC AND PRIVATE LIFE

If that kind of parallel defines the pattern of the Henry VI plays, the dramatic technique is more complicated from *Richard II* on. The principle of ethical similarity still holds,

2. symbolic   3. first four plays: *Henry VI*, Parts 1, 2, and 3 and *Richard III*

but Shakespeare turns part of his attention to other relationships between public and private life. As he comes to focus
on men striving and failing or succeeding in their effort to be
good kings, he explores the special pressure that being a
king puts on the man. As a result the two realms—public and
domestic—are no longer separate. In growing up and coming to terms with his father, Hal learns to be a king, and his
personal development is made especially difficult by his position as heir apparent and by his father's questionable title.

Richard III culminates Shakespeare's first experiments
with the history play. The three Henry VI plays are in a sense
stepping-stones toward its achievement, though that should
not obscure their independent merit. The chronicles gave
Shakespeare a large amount of varied material, and the orthodox view of history gave him a theme and a dramatic pattern. . . . It is apparent that two strands in dramatic tradition
offered some of the techniques that he needed: the largely
native morality play and the imported Senecan tragedy. . . .

THE FAMILY AND POLITICS

Although the first tetralogy concentrates on public affairs,
these two traditions provide a place for the family as a commentary on the political themes. The theme of inheritance is
a natural part of Shakespeare's chosen subject, since the
succession of the monarchy was the main element of
fifteenth-century history in which the Elizabethans saw
lessons for their own time. Also central to the history were
the great noble houses with their demands for loyalty often
conflicting with duty to the king. But even the elements of
family life that seem most detached from great public events
have an inner connection with them according to the doctrine of correspondences. Elizabethan audiences would notice that Henry VI's wife usurps the mastery in their marriage just as the Duke of York usurps the throne.

Still there are many other correspondences that can and
do provide similar parallels; another reason accounts for the
special prominence of the family. Politics was a matter of
great concern to every man when Spain and the Roman
Catholic church threatened England's life and the succession to the throne was in doubt, but even so politics was a
mysterious and distant subject to much of Shakespeare's audience in the popular theater. Issues of state came alive for
them when he showed their impact on the family. If ten

thousand spectators wept to see Talbot die, it must have been in part because they could imagine how a father and son dying together must feel. When Richard III scoffed at his mother's blessing, they were amused and shocked, but they were not puzzled.

Therefore the primary function of the family in these plays is analogical. It shows the value of political order and the consequences of its perversion. . . .

THE POWER OF ABSTRACT IDEAS IN *RICHARD III*

Mirror-scenes are useful in bringing to bear the full symbolic weight of the family. In the Henry VI plays they are more or less peripheral, reinforcing themes established elsewhere; but in *Richard III* the episodes involving the wailing women are essential to show the gradually increasing power working against Richard. At first the women seem as ineffectual as Henry VI on the battlefield of Towton, but the mysterious figure Queen Margaret brings the power to curse. Also, as the Duchess of York comes to dominate Anne and Elizabeth, her strength of character helps them to find a moral stance in opposition to Richard. These three women reassert the values of love and family loyalty. They express the moral order of which Richmond is the physical power. These scenes are less simply emblematic than those in the Henry VI plays, more a part of the dramatic whole.

Thus Shakespeare finds an important place for the family in this group of political plays. But since its function is mainly thematic, the tendency is toward abstraction and generalization. The nuances of a personal relationship are largely irrelevant to the broad moral issues that he is dramatizing. Hence he cultivates a style of lofty impressiveness at the cost of immediacy. . . . Something is lost to the family by associating it with this severe style. . . .

Richard III is a brilliant achievement in its own terms, but it is an idea-centered play. Despite the great vitality of its protagonist, the building-blocks of the play are concepts rather than characters. The play, indeed the whole tetralogy, succeeds because these concepts are woven into a rich and meaningful pattern, one in which even the striking figure of Richard Crookback has his place. Hereafter Shakespeare's dramatic art will take a new turn, but no other Elizabethan play excels *Richard III* in its own mode. There is room for a deeper exploration of the family, but Shakespeare must devise a new form for the history play to admit such exploration and adapt it to a political theme. If a character developed as fully as Richard and having his vitality of language were placed in the family, not isolated from it, a whole new range of potentiality would open up.

EXPERIMENTATION IN *KING JOHN* AND *RICHARD II*

King John and *Richard II* include some of Shakespeare's experimentation with the history play. In outline *King John* repeats some of the major themes of *Richard III*. It portrays an efficient usurper who loses control of events when his brutality toward the rightful heir to the throne mobilizes opinion against him. . . .

Richard II is another study of a weakly evil king, and it starts the chain of guilt that ends only with Richmond's victory in *Richard III*. Still the pattern of guilt and disorder is overshadowed by interest in Richard's character as he reacts to adversity. Of special importance for the next three histories is the concern with how Richard's official role affects his understanding of himself. Here Shakespeare takes up with new interest the relationship between the public and private man. It is not true, as romantic critics like Yeats argued, that Richard's vices are only political and that he is a creature too spiritual for the dirty work of governing men. His cruelty as a king manifests itself in part by an attack on his own family, and he shows no signs of genuine personal attachment to anyone, even after he is humbled by grief. But the isolation that he himself has chosen is painful to him, especially since it forces him to confront the truth of his fall without any support. His tragedy is that his failure to live up to his royal office destroys him as a man. . . .

THE EDUCATION OF PRINCE HAL
BRINGS FAMILY AND STATE TOGETHER

In the Henry IV plays Shakespeare finds a pattern that allows him to relate the family to the state without reverting to the simpler parallels of the first tetralogy. All the themes from Tudor orthodoxy are still there. Shakespeare constantly implies the need for order and for the extension of personal virtues like love and loyalty to the public realm. But in turning to a new theme, the education of a prince, he adapts a popular dramatic form built on the parable of the Prodigal Son. Christ's parable uses family life as a symbol of man's relationship to God, and so it is easily adapted to the multiple levels of Shakespeare's concern. Hal is a son who breaks away from his father but finally returns to take his place in the family. At the same time he is a prince who gains insight into his land by escaping the court and seeing the taverns and back roads. This escape involves the peril of weakening his position as heir to the throne, but on his return Hal takes up his heritage and even brings new strength to it. In his reconciliation with his father the king, he reaffirms his commitment to the principle of order. After his coronation he promises the man who has dared to judge even him with justice, "You shall be as a father to my youth" (*2 Henry IV*, V.ii.118).

Of all the characters in the two Henry IV plays, only Hal chooses the values of the family with complete integrity and comprehension of the issues involved. Some of the others offer verbal tribute, using the formal language of the first tetralogy, but their actions belie their commitment. Thus the Percies demonstrate their unworthiness for rule by their disloyalty to one another. Only Hotspur is unwavering in his fidelity to the common cause, and he keeps his integrity by a thorough blindness to his partners' motives. His simple chivalric code, both admirable and slightly comic, is all that holds the Percy rebellion together. When his father betrays him and lets him take the field at Shrewsbury against hopeless odds, his death ends the Percies' effective power. Hal, reconciled with Henry IV, kills Hotspur in a single combat that acts out their duel for moral supremacy.

Opposite Hotspur, Falstaff has the clown's prerogative of parodying everything in the serious plot, including the family themes. He is the old generation masquerading as youth, and he pretends to be a father to Hal who must pass on to him the code of moral inheritance. The inheritance he offers is the code of Puritan highwaymen. To the extent that Falstaff is joking, Hal can play his game; but there is a serious claim to influence and favor in the knight's manner that Hal must finally reject. Liberal education though his friendship is, Falstaff is also a tempter toward anarchy. Hal's ironic detachment allows him to enjoy Falstaff without succumbing to his influence. The fat knight is a father to Hal's youthful spirits, but not to his moral commitments.

Central to Hal's growth toward fitness for the monarchy are the two confrontations with his father—especially the second, when the old king is dying. Here Shakespeare dramatizes Hal's attainment of personal maturity and with it his acceptance of his public role. As Henry talks with his son, his clarity of vision is dimmed by age, sickness, and the pressure of maintaining himself on a doubtful throne; but his selfless concern with England's future shows him at his best. For all his guilt, Henry has both shrewdness and virtue for his son to inherit. Hal acts with propriety and affection to calm his father's doubts, but the intensity of his feeling suggests that the estrangement has been real enough. He has sought to escape the court in part because he knows the strain of being in authority. Hence he takes the crown from his father's bed with full consciousness of its burdens. Ironically, Henry completely misunderstands Hal's act, but his misunderstanding leads to the confrontation that clears the air between them. Henry can die in confidence that his son will carry on the Lancastrian heritage. He even hopes that Hal has escaped the guilt of Richard's deposition and death....

Hal's education occupies a central position between the political and comic plots, but it does not monopolize the interest of the plays. And even that theme allows for an extraordinary richness and complexity of development. Shown as it is in the Prodigal Son pattern, it includes psychological, political, and even religious meanings. It is as though Shakespeare turned to the other potentiality of correspondences so as to find multiple levels of meaning in one set of events.

SHAKESPEARE EXPLORES THE CONCEPT OF AN IDEAL KING

The central concern of the Henry IV plays is still political, but the political issues are seen in a broader and more human way than in the first tetralogy. The abstractions of Tudor orthodoxy are less important than the problem of how a man can live up to his divinely appointed role. Shakespeare has given these doctrines a new depth by showing the human meaning of the great abstractions: order, majesty, patriotism, inherited nobility.

In *Henry V* Shakespeare undertakes to set forth an orderly state under an ideal king and to show that state conquering a mighty rival by the sheer impact of its virtue. Henry V is able to draw England together into a harmony and vigor that the French cannot rival. Such a theme being central, the family is not a primary concern, at least in the full development of the Henry IV plays. However, Shakespeare uses it as a public symbol, a touchstone by which to test the comparative merit of the English and the French, including their governors. Henry embodies the private virtues as well as the public, and the disorderly squabbles of the French king and the Dauphin illustrate the decay of the French commonweal.

Still *Henry V* is more than a political pageant. Henry himself is not just another Talbot because Shakespeare no longer allows his hero to have a merely public existence. However, it is through comradeship in arms rather than family life that we see most deeply into Henry's personal feelings. Much of his behavior is formal and public; only on the night before Agincourt does he reveal himself with the fullness of Shakespeare's mature craft. Powerful though that scene is and for all the exhilaration of the battle scenes, *Henry V* is a less interesting play than its two historical predecessors. Perhaps one reason is its return to a simpler and more formal way of using the family.

One conclusion should be apparent if this analysis is valid: the family as part of man's personal life is not opposed to what is needed for success in public affairs. It is true that a king must lose the sense of personal contact with others which private men can feel and that Shakespeare finds a deep pathos in this loss. However, the family can serve as an analogy to the state precisely because their ethics are parallel. It is the school of political nobility and skill, and it suffers when the governors of the commonwealth lack virtue. Because it and the state are parts of a larger organism, their healths are interdependent. This doctrine allows Shakespeare to develop a dramatic technique that modulates between the public and private worlds. His plays can have both scope and unity because he sees a larger unity in the nature to which he holds up the mirror. But the metaphysic of correspondences does not offer a dramatic technique fully developed for his use. His growth as a craftsman during the 1590s is in part an expansion of scope to take in more and more of man's life without losing unity and control. One side of that growth comes through the history plays as he learns to illuminate both the family and the political world by their relation to each other.

Women in the History Plays

Linda Bamber

Linda Bamber argues that Isabel in *Richard II* is
Shakespeare's only completely feminine character.
Bamber maintains that before Isabel, Joan of Arc
(*1 Henry VI*) is essentially a second-class man and
after Isabel, women are portrayed as mere adjuncts to
men. None of the women in the histories, she concludes, acts with enough force to influence men or
their actions. Linda Bamber, who has taught at Tufts
University in Medford, Massachusetts, has extensively
researched gender roles in Shakespeare's plays.

In the two tetralogies[1] of English history plays, the feminine
Other[2] seems to change as we go along. From the beginning
of the first tetralogy to the first play of the second, the desires
and activities of women are differentiated more and more
from those of the men. My series begins with Joan of Arc in
1 Henry VI and ends with Isabel in *Richard II;* Joan is in
many ways similar to the masculine Self, whereas Isabel is
very different. The masculine Self in history is always defined in terms of his place in the world of men. His central
activity is the struggle to procure, maintain, or wield power,
and his experience of what lies beyond this struggle is limited. At the beginning of the history cycles the woman is also
defined in terms of her success or failure in the masculine-
historical struggle for power. Joan of Arc fights and kills like
a man, desires only victory for her party and power for herself. Isabel, at the other end of my series, embodies an idea
of the feminine that is fully differentiated from the masculine Self. She is queen of an alternative realm, the realm of
the garden where her major scene takes place. The world of

1. the first and second sets of four plays   2. a female type as distinguished from a male
type

Reprinted from *Comic Women, Tragic Men: A Study of Gender and Genre in Shakespeare,* by Linda Bamber, with the permission of the publishers, Stanford University
Press; ©1982 by the Board of Trustees of the Leland Stanford Junior University.

men offers political and military adventure and a headlong struggle for power; Isabel's garden world is private, slow, full of a sorrow that cannot be released in action. In the histories the feminine develops from an almost undifferentiated participant in the masculine adventure into an emblem of what is left out in the masculine-historical mode. Initially similar to the masculine Self, the feminine changes into something essentially different. . . .

ISABEL'S FEMININE IDENTITY

The one female character in these plays who is defined by something beyond history is Queen Isabel in *Richard II*. Isabel's sense of loss is resonant with more than the fortunes of the political moment. Indeed, in Act II, scene ii, she grieves a loss that has not yet occurred:

> Some unborn sorrow ripe in Fortune's womb
> Is coming towards me; and my inward soul
> With nothing trembles—at something it grieves
> More than with parting from my lord the king.

(II.ii.10–13)

The conversation in which this speech occurs is itself an anomaly in a history play—leisurely, philosophical, dealing with the nature of emotion. Furthermore, Isabel rejects Bushy's[3] commonsense analysis and insists on the reality of her 'inward soul' and its feelings. It is not merely Richard's departure that she grieves, as Bushy supposes, but something hidden, mysterious, ineffable. Isabel alone of the history women connects us to this intangible world.

With Isabel's crucial scenes we get a sense of stop-action, a quick descent into a different world. Time moves differently when we are with her; nothing happens. It is the garden scene that most strikingly illustrates the alternative Isabel represents. Here we are aware of natural time, not historical time; of the growth of plants rather than the movement of the wheel of Fortune. The Queen, of course, is not the one who talks of grafting, pruning and binding the flowers. But it is she who supplies the emotion in this scene, and her emotion at the news of Richard's demise is what forges the bond between man and the natural things in the garden. As she leaves she says, 'Gard'ner, for telling me these news of woe, / Pray God, the plants thou graft'st may never grow'

---

3. Bushy is servant to King Richard

(III.iv.100–1). He answers,

> Poor queen, so that thy state might be no worse,
> I would my skill were subject to thy curse.
> Here did she fall a tear; here in this place
> I'll set a bank of rue, sour herb of grace;
> Rue even for ruth [pity] here shortly shall be seen,
> In the remembrance of a weeping queen.
>
> (III.iv.102–7)

The symbolic connection between the woman and the flower, even though it is unhappy, creates a sense of a female principle apart from history. Like Ophelia and Perdita[4] distributing flowers, Isabel in the garden reminds us of our place in nature, which, unlike our place in society, is not subject to the wheel of time. Isabel's grief interrupts the momentum of the action; it surrounds Richard's downfall like a nimbus of sorrowful love.

ISABEL RESEMBLES WOMEN IN TRAGEDIES

With Isabel we arrive at an idea of the feminine similar to the one that operates in the tragedies. For the feminine in the tragedies is associated with unhistorical experience. From one point of view, of course, this is a pity. At one level, the progression I have been describing is nothing but a progression toward the cultural stereotype. Isabel is passive whereas the typical history hero is active; while she grieves, he fights. A feminine defined in terms of gardens, the ineffable, and natural cycles of time is certainly nothing new. What we are missing are images of women who *do* participate in history, and the progression I have been describing may seem to be a movement away from the feminine as an element in history. But the women in the early history plays do not participate in history *as women*. Joan is a kind of second-class man. . . . Since such characters participate in history only as inferior versions of the masculine Self, or as failed versions of the feminine Other, they do not offer the kind of images we might profit from. The women characters in these plays who are involved in the events of history either betray their own femininity or simply mimic the men. Nothing is lost, then, in the progression from Joan to Isabel. And from the perspective of what is to follow the histories, something is gained. For in the tragedies, the woman as Other becomes a powerful dialectical force, and the progres-

4. Ophelia is a young woman in *Hamlet*, Perdita in *The Winter's Tale*

sion toward Isabel is a progression toward feminine Otherness. The separation of Isabel from the world of men prefigures the dialectical opposition in the tragedies between the world of men and the woman as Other. Only as the Other are women in Shakespeare consistently the equals of men. Only in opposition to the hero and the world of men, only as representatives of alternative experience do the women characters matter to Shakespeare's drama as much as the men.

In the tragedies the women characters oppose the world of men in several ways. Sometimes they represent an antihistorical world; sometimes they directly threaten the hero's place in history; sometimes they simply elicit such powerful and chaotic emotions from the hero that he can no longer play his public role. . . . The feminine in the tragedies is always something that cannot be possessed, controlled, conquered; it resists the colonising impulse of the imperial male Self. . . .

CHALLENGING WOMEN OMITTED FROM HISTORIES

But in *Richard II* the challenge of Isabel's Otherness is only latent. The feminine offers too powerful a challenge to the idea of history itself for Shakespeare to deal with it in the history plays. The Otherness of the feminine challenges the ethos of power and conquest through aggression; history as a genre must ultimately base itself on that ethos no matter how it also criticises it. If we lose interest in the military-political adventure we have lost interest in history itself as a genre. The feminine is not the only challenge to the history ethos; the struggle for power in Shakespearean history is always as tawdry as it is glamorous, challenged by common sense, common decency, and a sense of the common good. But apparently there is something uncommon in the challenge offered by the feminine. The feminine Other is too explosive a figure for history; having arrived, with Isabel, at a feminine that is truly Other, Shakespeare seems to put her away for safekeeping until he is ready to abandon history for tragedy. Not until he is ready to abandon history altogether does the feminine return in force.

After Isabel, the women characters neither participate in history nor challenge it. They merely create a kind of contrast or background from which the hero rides off to his adventure. Hotspur's parting from his wife is illustrative. In *1 Henry IV* Lady Percy tries to get a declaration of love from Hotspur as he is leaving her for the wars; he replies,

> Come, wilt thou see me ride?
> And when I am a-horseback,
> I will swear I love thee infinitely.
>
> (II.iii.99–101)

Shakespeare seems to have understood the implications of history-as-a-genre for relations with women, and here presents them in their starkest form. If women neither seriously challenge the values of the history world nor participate as women in the crucial activities of this world, then they are supernumeraries in a world of men. Relations with the feminine take place but do not much matter: 'This is no world', as Hotspur puts it, 'To play with mammets[5] and to tilt with lips'[6] (II.iii.90–1). If the woman is not a version of the Other, she is powerless to counteract the lure of the masculine-historical adventure. Hotspur, the true believer in history-as-an-ethos, demonstrates the irrelevance of the feminine to those who live up to this creed. Kate's response to Hotspur's rejection is illuminating:

> Do you not love me? Do you not indeed?
> Well, do not then; for since you love me not,
> I will not love myself. Do you not love me?
> Nay, tell me if you speak in jest or no.
>
> (II.iii.95–8)

Where the woman does not represent the Other, she is and perceives herself to be merely the adjunct of the man. She has no kingdom of her own, and if he abandons her she loses everything.

HENRY V IS UNAFFECTED BY KATHERINE

Of course, Hotspur and Kate are only one version of relations between men and women in the last three plays of the second tetralogy. A more significant version, perhaps, is the one represented by Henry V and Katherine of France. For Hotspur only represents history at its most unselfconscious, and therefore he verges on self-parody. Henry V is the opposite of Hotspur; he is thoroughly conscious of his own role as a history hero, as detached as can be from his role. But even Henry V is not confronted by the feminine Other. Katherine is no challenge to Henry's public role.

As one critic has put it, 'Katherine is regarded by everybody (including herself), and by Henry in the first place, as part of the war spoils resulting from the Agincourt victory.'

5. dolls   6. kiss

Henry may love Katherine, as he says he does, but she is no more serious an issue for him than Kate is for Hotspur. . . .

HENRY V EASILY WINS KATHERINE

Katherine of France, however, is no representative of the feminine that ends history. When women represent a significant challenge to the masculine-historical mode, the heroes are never so good-humoured as Henry is in his relations with Katherine. The great final wooing scene in *Henry V* is the most sustained encounter between a man and a woman in the histories, and it is worth looking at in some detail.

The most notable feature of this scene is the complete absence of anxiety with which this great hero of history approaches the feminine. Henry is relaxed and self-confident, animated by an enjoyment of his own performance. He begins with a little easy hyperbole: 'An angel is like you Kate, and you are like an angel' (V.ii.110–11). But things aren't going to be *that* easy. Katherine protests against the obvious flattery by murmuring something about language and deception; so Henry immediately switches to the plain style:

> I know no ways to mince it in love, but directly to say, 'I love you'. Then, if you urge me farther than to say, 'Do you swear in faith?' I wear out my suit. Give me your answer, i' faith, do; and so clap hands, and a bargain. How say you, lady?
>
> (V.ii.128–33)

If Kate wants plainness, Henry seems to say, how is 'clap hands, and a bargain' for plainness? Obviously, a little too plain. Henry will not be trapped into sincerity, even though his love may be sincere. His bluffness is a role he plays to reveal and conceal himself simultaneously. He does want to win Katherine of France, but he also knows he has already won her—at Agincourt. The bluffness is a way of being true to both these facts:

> I speak to thee plain soldier: if thou canst love me for this, take me, if not, to say to thee that I shall die, is true—but for thy love, by the Lord, no; yet I love thee too.
>
> (V.ii.152–5)

Henry's feelings are clear enough—to himself, to Katherine, and to us. . . .

Henry's speeches go wittily on and on, turning corners, leaping fences, backing into antitheses—while Katherine confines herself to dimples and coyness. Of Henry's insolent French, for instance, she says primly and conventionally,

'Sauf votre honneur, le français que vous parlez, il est meilleur que l'anglais lequel je parle'[7] (V.ii.190–1). A heroine with the substance to challenge male strengths—a Desdemona or a Cleopatra—would never meet Henry's provocation with so mild and straight a response.

'Strain' and 'effort' are precisely what this scene is free of. Henry's power and desire is wholly unopposed by Katherine, who is a negligible presence in the scene. Henry has all the good lines. If this scene is the right one to 'cap' the play, as [critic Michael] Goldman says, it is because Henry at ease is as compelling as Henry at his real work, not because Henry works as hard to play the lover as he does to play the general. The opposition by the French troops was real and dangerous; Katherine's opposition is non-existent. Neither Hotspur's Kate nor Henry's Katherine offers any resistance to the exercise of masculine power. . . .

From Joan to Isabel, then, the feminine in history follows a progression away from second-class citizenship in the world of men and toward a separate identity; but as soon as Shakespeare establishes the separateness of the feminine, he shelves the feminine as an Other until he is ready to write tragedy. The challenge of the feminine would destroy the historical mode; or, to put it the other way around, when Shakespeare is finished with history and ready for tragedy, the challenge of the feminine, heretofore latent, suddenly becomes central to his drama.

7. Except your honor, the French that you speak is better than the English that I speak.

The History Plays on Stage

George J. Becker

George J. Becker describes the Elizabethan play-house, the limitations it imposed on production of the history plays as well as the opportunities it afforded. Becker then compares Elizabethan staging with important movie versions and modern American, Canadian, and British repertory theater productions of the history plays. George J. Becker, who taught English at Swathmore College, is well known as a translator of Jean-Paul Sartre's works and as the editor and translator of *Documents of Modern Literary Realism.*

Our notions about production in Shakespeare's day are mainly inferential, based on what we know, or think we know, about the theatrical companies and the stages that they used. Both the makeup of the companies and their stages, in fact, had an important part in the way plays were put together as well as in the way they were presented.

Shakespeare's company and its rivals were what we now call repertory groups, in which the senior members were theoretically equal and could therefore expect adequate opportunities for their particular talents as actors. There definitely was not a star system, though it is true that in Shakespeare's company the great roles of the tragedies (and of Richard III) seem to have been reserved for Richard Burbage. The necessity to cater to the requirements of fellow actors is in itself enough to account for the comic scenes in serious plays. One can hear an actor asking the dramatist about the play he is working on: "What's in it for me, Will?" and imagine his complaints if he is too long relegated to the sidelines. The greater variety of roles provided by the comic sequences in *2 Henry VI*, for example, suggests Shakespeare's attempt to meet such complaints as he worked his way into the new genre of the history play.

PRODUCTION PROBLEMS AND LIMITATIONS

There was also an innate limitation by reason of the use of boys to take women's parts, a limitation that extended to the whole range of Elizabethan and Jacobean[1] drama. No play has many female parts, presumably because no company had many apprentices capable of taking on such roles. The only stellar female role in all of Shakespeare is that of Cleopatra. In the histories, only the roles of Queen Margaret in the Henry VI plays and Queen Katherine in *Henry VIII* approach major dimensions. Shakespeare's most common practice, however, was to handle female roles so that continuing presence on stage and sustained acting were not demanded.

The physical limitations and peculiarities of the Elizabethan stage are another shaping factor. In all the histories except *Henry VIII* there is military action. Yet no stage is big enough to give a sense of the massive encounter of two armies. Thus the fighting has to be reduced to the level of individual combat in a rapid succession of personal encounters as the sword-wielding combatants run on and off stage parrying each other's blows. Repeated movement has to substitute for mass.

The amusing, if vexing, problem of how to dispose of bodies also had its effect on the plays. Since in the Elizabethan theater and its modern counterpart there was no curtain to be rung down, the bodies had to be removed by the actors on scene, as we see in the tragedies and histories alike. Hamlet lugs off Polonius after he has stabbed him through the arras. Falstaff shoulders the dead Hotspur, whom he claims as his victim. Henry IV is led off scene so that he can die in the Jerusalem chamber.[2] After Richard II is killed, there are three bodies to dispose of. The stage direction is contained in the text as Exton orders that the two servants be carried off for burial and himself undertakes to bear "the dead king to the living king." Similarly, after killing Jack Cade, Iden tells us that he will drag Cade away and then cut off his head. Sometimes after mass carnage there is an awkward heaving up of many bodies by attendant lords and soldiers before the

---

1. the reign of James I, 1603–1625   2. The abbot's parlor in the monastic buildings of Westminster Abbey, the scene of the conspiracy against Henry IV and of his death

action can continue. For this reason, a good many killings are done off stage. A bloody severed head triumphantly brought *on* stage as evidence is easier to handle than a dead body. The theater property rooms must have been well supplied with dummy heads.

THE ELIZABETHAN PLAYHOUSE

The physical conformation of the Elizabethan playhouse had its influence on the staging of a play. Not only was there no curtain, there was no scenery, and there were virtually no properties. Thus the action was continuous, without waits for scene-shifting. If necessary, change of place was indicated by the lines themselves; most frequently it did not matter or could be inferred from who was on stage. Plays that in the nineteenth- and twentieth-century era of elaborate settings needed four hours for presentation occupied much less time, could be performed uncut, and had the further advantage of rapidity of action.

The stage itself was a rectangle—an apron—wider than it was deep, jutting out into the audience. Dressing rooms may have been beneath it. Entrances and exits took place from the sides at the back. Behind the stage was a permanent three-story structure that masked behind-the-scenes activity and permitted some variety in deploying actors and creating a stage picture. On ground level was an inner chamber that could apparently be shut off by a tapestry, the pulling back of which permitted a character to be "discovered," as in the case of King Claudius at prayer in *Hamlet* or Falstaff fast asleep after the sheriff's visit in *1 Henry IV.* This concealment made it possible to set up more elaborate and individualized scenes than were possible on the forestage. There is difference of opinion, however, as to whether actions of any great duration could go on in this recess because of the problem of voice projection.

At the second-story level was a balcony—perhaps a catwalk would be a better description—which permitted action to go on at two levels at once. It is from this elevation that the gunner's boy shoots Salisbury in *1 Henry VI.* It is there that Richard III stands between two holy bishops as he waits to be entreated to take the crown. It is from there that Richard II, after a colloquy[3] with Aumerle, descends to the courtyard

3. a conversation or dialogue

in capitulation to Bolingbroke. There was additionally a parapet at the top of the background structure that could also be used, though perhaps only for ceremonial purposes. It is at one of these upper levels that inhabitants of besieged towns shout defiance and the victors show themselves in flag-waving jubilation. It is there that heads of traitors are impaled.

The stage itself had a number of trapdoors, particularly useful for the appearance and disappearance of spirits. In *King John* when young Arthur jumps to his death, it is through one of these traps. In spite of such useful variations, most of the action took place on the stage proper, at about the eye level of spectators standing in the pit, without sets and with only the scantiest properties. We must remember too that these plays were performed in daylight (at the popular theaters), so that torches, the only kind of lighting available, had minimal effect. It was a spare and spartan setting for the vast enterprises of history, as the Chorus admits at the beginning of *Henry V*, when he entreats the audience:

Still be kind,
And eke out our performance with your mind.

THE HISTORIES AS SPECTACLE

Nonetheless, history plays in particular afford opportunities for spectacle. The presence of kings and nobles connotes elaborate ritual and pageantry. Kings rarely move about unattended or, on the Elizabethan stage, uncrowned. Pomp attends them with torches, banners, trumpets, heralds, and gorgeously appareled courtiers and knights at arms. Thus even on the Elizabethan stage there were many opportunities to dazzle the eye of the beholder, and, producers being what they are, there is every reason to believe that they took advantage of those opportunities, on occasion subordinating action to sheer spectacle.

Their chief resource was costume. In Shakespeare's day it was the custom for actors to wear contemporary costume, a convention that, in fact, continued until the early nineteenth century, when the romantic cult of the past encouraged the innovation of costuming for period. In the eighteenth century, for example, John Philip Kemble played Richard III in silk knee breeches, and so did David Garrick. On Shakespeare's stage, the actors were strutting peacocks, bearing their rather meager fortunes on their backs but thereby lending brilliance to the scene.

The acting, so far as we can judge, was stylized and declamatory, as is attested by the number of set speeches in many of the plays, especially the early histories. Speeches of seventy lines or more are not uncommon, and they were probably not much alleviated by business on the part of background characters. It is likely that for certain of the major roles long-continuing conventions of interpretation and costume existed. To cite one example, after the theaters reopened in 1660, continuity with Shakespeare's age was maintained by reliance on the recollection and advice of "old Mr. Lowin," that is, John Lowin, who was an interpreter of Falstaff during Shakespeare's lifetime and who lived on until 1653.

However, the eighteen-year-long closing of the theaters from 1642 to 1660, imposed by the Puritan Commonwealth, did break continuity in certain important respects. After the reopening women were permitted to take female roles. The star system became increasingly important. The theaters themselves changed their appearance and capacities with the advent of the proscenium-arch stage. Shakespeare's histories were largely out of favor, partly because of their mixture of genres, partly because of the increasing remoteness of the Wars of the Roses, and partly because they did not offer many stellar roles. It was the actor Thomas Betterton who kept Shakespeare alive after the Restoration;[4] he played Hotspur and Falstaff among other roles. Samuel Pepys noted in his diary that he saw *Henry V* on December 28, 1666.

In 1700 a version of *Richard III* put together by [playwright] Colley Cibber began a career on the boards that lasted for two centuries. During that period, when the great Shakespearean actors went in for heavy roles, among the histories *Richard III* was far and above their favorite. Virtually every actor of note essayed it—in Cibber's version. This was a concoction that drew from *3 Henry VI*, the plays of the Henriad, *Richard III*, and Cibber's own imagination. For generations playgoers quoted the line "Off with his head! So much for Buckingham" with relish as one of Shakespeare's finest touches. It is, of course, by Cibber, but apparently few people knew the difference. . . .

4. the period of British history between the crowning of Charles II in 1660 and the Glorious Revolution in 1688

THE HISTORY PLAYS IN THE TWENTIETH CENTURY

Inevitably this taste for the spectacular was translated to the screen. A very early movie (1914) starred "The Eminent Tragedian Mr. Frederick Warde in Shakespeare's Play Richard III. Five reels—5000 feet—a Feature Costing $30,000 to Produce." This landmark production used 1500 people, 200 horses, and a three-masted warship. It was acclaimed at the time as excelling anything the stage could do, though it was only an amateur precursor of Laurence Olivier's stunning film of *Richard III* (1955), in which the battle scenes, filmed in Spain, had full scope. However, Olivier continued the early tradition of playing ducks and drakes with Shakespeare's text, leaving out Queen Margaret and drawing elements from *3 Henry VI* and from the Cibber version.

It is in the last fifty years that the histories have come into their own through a fortunate combination of circumstances: the foundation of repertory theaters devoted to producing Shakespeare and the emergence of an unusual number of exceptional actors who are sensitive to the needs of such productions and willing to subordinate their talents to them.

In point of fact, the spring festivals at Stratford-on-Avon began in 1879. The first history put on there, in 1883, was *1 Henry IV*. In the next sixty years *Henry V* and *Richard II* were the histories most often presented, followed fairly closely by *Richard III* and the two parts of *Henry IV*. . . .

For the 1951 Festival of Britain the Stratford company put on the plays of the second tetralogy—*Richard II*, *1 Henry IV*, *2 Henry IV*, and *Henry V*—in sequence, the first time this had been done since 1905. It was a remarkable gathering together of talent: Anthony Quayle as Falstaff, Richard Burton as Prince Hal/Henry V, and Michael Redgrave as Richard II and the Chorus in *Henry V*. The Old Vic, the Memorial Theater's London competitor, did all of Shakespeare's plays between 1914 and 1923, and with the omission of *Pericles* ran through them again in 1953 through 1958. . . .

Not only did the Stratford-on-Avon theater and the Old Vic (as well as the New Old Vic) in London make it a practice to present the complete canon of Shakespeare's plays, but other companies came into being with the same goals. The Birmingham Repertory Company in England, the Festival Theater at Stratford, Ontario, the American Festival Theater at Stratford, Connecticut (which came to an end in 1976), and the Oregon Festival Theater at Ashland, Oregon, have all, for periods ranging over two to four decades, put on Shakespearean seasons. The result is that almost anyone who has wanted to in England has been able to see all the histories, and that North Americans, east and west, have, with a little more effort and expense, had the same opportunity. . . .

Although modern productions have been much more faithful to the texts and to Elizabethan conventions of staging than their predecessors, they have not escaped gimmickry. A production of *Henry V* at the First Mermaid Theater in London in 1960 succumbed to the vogue for modern dress. Hal greeted the Archbishop of Canterbury in cricket flannels; the battle dress was updated; and the Chorus attempted a rendition of "Roses of Picardy" on the mouth-organ. A recent production of *King John* invested John's death with the solemnity of a chanting procession of monks—singularly inappropriate considering the reputed cause of his death.

The unprecedented availability of the histories on stage is not proof absolute of renewed interest on the part of audiences. Shakespeare has become big business at the Stratfords and at Ashland. Though it can be noticed that the attention of spectators frequently wanders and that entr'acte conversations sometimes express more bewilderment than understanding, still the audiences keep coming—even to *Henry VI*. It is likely that beneath the pomp and the recondite events of these plays audiences do discern relevance to the twentieth century. Our power struggles are not dynastic, and they are on a scale inconceivable to the adherents of York and Lancaster. Still if we are sometimes confused by the details of those ancient conflicts, they do show the age-old maneuvers of men who have power, who lose it, or who try to gain it. Just as *Coriolanus* has become popular in our time, because it deals with problems of dictatorship, so the English histories have an interest for twentieth-century audiences. . . .

Social disaster in our day is so vast as to be incommensurable; it dwarfs victims and victimizers alike. It is mechanical, nonhuman, unintelligible. But the social disasters Shakespeare portrays are on a smaller scale. Men are the agents of their own destruction or redemption. Their motives are recognizable Their power has manifest limits. Above all they inhabit a moral universe. Though intellectually we may scoff at such a providential view of history as simple, even shallow, emotionally we respond to it and find comfort in it.

CHAPTER 2

The Richard Plays

READINGS ON
THE HISTORIES

Abuse and Neglect of Power in *Richard II*

L.C. Knights

According to L.C. Knights, *Richard II* shows the consequences of both the abuse of power and the neglect of it. Richard II, a brutal and unjust king, deceives himself about his divine right to the kingship and neglects the threat from his usurper, Bolingbroke. Consequently, he loses his crown and his life. L.C. Knights has taught English at the University of Manchester and Cambridge University in England. He is the author of *How Many Children Had Lady Macbeth?*, *Shakespeare's Politics*, and *Some Shakespeare Themes*.

Richard II (1595) is a political play with a difference. Drawing on events known to everyone as leading to the English civil wars of the fifteenth century, it presents a political fable of permanent interest: for what it shows is how power—hardly conscious of its own intentions until the event fulfills them—must necessarily fill a vacuum caused by the withdrawal of power. But behind the public framework attention is concentrated on *the kind of man* who plays the central role. Richard is more than an unkingly king, he is an egotist who, like egotists in humbler spheres, constructs an unreal world that finally collapses about him. And it is because the political interest cannot be separated from the psychological interest—is indeed dependent on it—that *Richard II* is a different kind of play from *King John:* in some important ways it looks back to *Richard III*[1] and forward to *Julius Caesar* and *Macbeth*.

RICHARD'S UNJUST AND BRUTAL NATURE

That Richard is a king, and not simply a man, and that the play is about the deposition of a king—these are cardinal

1. Shakespeare wrote *Richard III* in 1592–93, *Richard II* in 1594–95.

Reprinted from *William Shakespeare: The Histories:* Richard III, King John, Richard II, Henry V, by L.C. Knights (London: Longmans, Green & Co., 1962).

dramatic facts; and most of Richard's actions have to do with the exercise of kingly power, or the failure to exercise it. What we should think of the King the play leaves in no doubt. Of the king-becoming graces named in *Macbeth* Justice stands first, and Richard is not just. The matter of Gloucester's death though referred to with some explicitness, lies outside the action of the play, but the whole of the first two acts portrays an arbitrariness and self-will that respects neither persons nor established rights. Richard is an extortionate landlord of his realm; he is brutal and unjust towards Gaunt; and in depriving Bolingbroke of his inheritance he strikes at the foundations of his own power:

> Take Hereford's rights away, and take from time
> His charters and his customary rights;
> Let not tomorrow then unsue to-day;
> Be not thyself; for how art thou a king
> But by fair sequence and succession?
>
> (II.ii.195–9)

Action is reinforced by explicit commentary. Richard's behaviour is a 'rash fierce blaze of riot'; it is 'vanity'; it is a 'surfeit' that will inevitably bring its 'sick hour'. At the turning point of the action the gardeners are introduced for no other purpose than to moralize the event:

> *First Servant.* Why should we, in the compass of a pale,
> Keep law and form and due proportion,
> Showing, as in a model, our firm estate,
> When our sea-walled garden, the whole land,
> Is full of weeds? . . .
> *Gardener.*   Hold thy peace—
> He that hath suffered this disordered spring
> Hath now himself met with the fall of leaf . . .
>   . . . and Bolingbroke
> Hath seiz'd the wasteful king. O, what pity is it
> That he had not so trimm'd and dress'd this land
> As we this garden! . . .
>   Superfluous branches
> We lop away, that bearing boughs may live;
> Had he done so, himself had borne the crown,
> Which waste of idle hours hath quite thrown down.[2]
>
> (III.iv.40ff.)

If however, according to Brents Stirling, 'the political moral of *Richard II* is clear . . . it is not simple'. Richard's misdeeds do not justify his deposition—and this not because Shake-

---

2. It is a mistake to play this scene as a simple mixture of humour and pathos: the Gardener, who is not a stage rustic, has a genuine 'authority'.

speare has passively accepted the doctrine of the sanctity of kingship and the sinfulness of rebellion. Gaunt, it is true, proclaims passive obedience before 'God's substitute, His deputy anointed in His sight', but this is balanced by the unavoidable questions prompted by Richard's own development of the theory of divine right. What guides us here is simply Shakespeare's appraisal of necessary consequences. It may be argued that Carlisle's impassioned prophecy before the deposition is prophecy only in appearance—Shakespeare had read Holinshed and knew what happened in the fifteenth century. But Shakespeare is not merely offering wisdom after the event; he is intent on causes and consequences, on the laws of human behaviour, as in Richard's rebuke to Northumberland after the deposition:

> thou shalt think,
> Though he divide the realm and give thee half,
> It is too little, helping him to all. . . .
> The love of wicked men converts to fear,
> That fear to hate. . . .
>
> (V.i.60ff.)

This is the way things happen in the game of power, and although Bolingbroke returns initially to claim what is justly his, he is no more—even if, confronting Richard's 'vanity', he is no less—than a man of power. In short, the play presupposes no possibility of a simple solution to the political situation: as Rossiter says, 'Richard is wrong, but Bolingbroke's coronation is not right; and Richard's murder converts it to the blackest wrong'. York's words apply to *both* sides—'To find out right with wrong—it may not be'.

RICHARD'S SELF-DECEPTION

Within this clearly delineated framework of a political dilemma—this soberly realistic mapping of one of history's cunning passages—interest centres on the man who is Richard II. He is early shown as petulant and wilful; but what the play focuses with especial clarity is the fact that he is a self-deceiver, a man who imagines that a habitable world can be constructed from words alone. As with many figures in the later plays, essential attitudes are embodied in a manner of speech which simultaneously 'places' them. On Richard's return from Ireland some sixty lines are devoted to this purpose alone:

> I weep for joy
> To stand upon my kingdom once again.

Dear earth, I do salute thee with my hand,
Though rebels wound thee with their horses' hoofs.
As a long-parted mother with her child
Plays fondly with her tears and smiles in meeting,
So weeping, smiling, greet I thee, my earth,
And do thee favours with my royal hands;
Feed not thy sovereign's foe, my gentle earth,
Nor with thy sweets comfort his ravenous sense,
But let thy spiders that suck up thy venom
And heavy-gaited toads lie in their way,
Doing annoyance to the treacherous feet,
Which with usurping steps do trample thee;
Yield stinging nettles to mine enemies

(III.ii.4ff.)

—and so on. There follows Richard's elaborate comparison of the king to the sun, leading into an assertion of divine right:

Not all the water in the rough rude sea
Can wash the balm off from an anointed king:
The breath of worldly men cannot depose
The deputy elected by the Lord;
For every man that Bolingbroke hath press'd
To lift shrewd steel against our golden crown,
God for his Richard hath in heavenly pay
A glorious angel.

(III.ii.54ff.)

The sequence prompts various reflections. Most obviously Richard has not been a 'mother' to his land (we last saw him ordering the seizure of Bolingbroke's possessions, and we have been told of his other exactions): this bit of make-believe is almost as fantastic as the notion that Bolingbroke would be troubled by spiders. Richard of course does not expect to be taken seriously—'Mock not my senseless conjuration, lords', he says: the trouble is that it is impossible to draw a line between this fanciful self-dramatization and the more seriously intended assertion of royal power that follows. Not only does the repeated use of the first person singular ('my earth' !) undermine the royal 'we' when it appears, Richard's assumption that heavenly powers will aid a king is seen, in this context, as not very different from the admittedly fanciful invocation of the English soil; indeed the religious references—as with the 'three Judases' later—only serve to underline the fearful discrepancy between Richard's self-deceiving rhetoric and reality. On a later speech in which self-dramatization is followed by foolish and irrelevant fantasy Dr. Johnson commented, 'Shakespeare is very apt to deviate from the pathetic to the ridiculous'; but it is Richard, not Shakespeare, who thus deviates.

THE CONSEQUENCES OF SELF-DECEPTION

Shakespeare however is using the figure of Richard for a more serious purpose than the exhibition of a particular kind of kingly incompetence. *Richard II* is not universal tragedy, as *Macbeth* is; nevertheless what lifts it above the previous political plays is the way in which reality breaks into the closed world of the self-deceiver. The deposition scene begins equivocally: there is dignity and pathos, but there is also the familiar self-regarding dramatization and habit of word-play. It is at the end of a passage of restrained rhetoric—beginning, characteristically, 'Now, mark me how I will undo myself'—that the process of recognition begins. There is indeed no sudden illumination, and the process is difficult to define without extensive quotation, but there is something that can properly be called a break-through from the depths of the nature that Shakespeare has imagined. It can be felt in the changed tone. Whereas Richard's earlier manner had been almost feminine, it is now masculine and direct. At the end of Richard's speech of self-deposition, the question, 'What more remains?' may be read as 'exhausted' or as an abrupt descent from rhetoric. What can be in no doubt is that from now on Richard sees himself without disguise:

> Must I do so? and must I ravel out
> My weaved-up follies? . . .
> Nay, if I turn mine eyes upon myself,
> I find myself a traitor with the rest. . . .
>   . . . I'll read enough
> When I do see the very book indeed
> Where all my sins are writ, and that's myself.
>
> (IV.i.228ff.)

It is this new tone that underprops the pathos ('Mine eyes are full of tears, I cannot see'), and makes the subsequent play with the mirror something different from mere self-indulgent theatricality: as Derek Traversi says, 'artificiality, conscious self-exhibition, and true self-exploration are typically blended':

> Was this the face
> That every day under his household roof
> Did keep ten thousand men? Was this the face
> That like the sun did make beholders wink?
> *Was this the face that faced* [trimmed] *so many follies.*
>
> (IV.i.281ff.)

In more senses than one Richard is a man at bay, for he is exposed to himself as well as to his enemies. It is a bleak awakening, as he admits with a sparse directness in the moving scene of his parting from his wife:

> Learn, good soul,
> To think our former state a happy dream;
> From which awak'd, the truth of what we are
> Shows us but this.

Richard still *sees* his own story; but he also sees his own 'profane hours', and the verse in which he foretells to Northumberland the consequences of usurpation is unusually forthright.

RICHARD FACES REALITY

The scene of the murder firmly establishes this new movement. Richard's thought is still fanciful (something not unlikely in solitary confinement) and his expression 'conceited'; but the more fanciful passages end with a return to the idiomatic and forthright:

> While I stand fooling here, his Jack o'the clock. . . .
> Spurr'd, gall'd, and tir'd by jauncing Bolingbroke;

and there is no turning away from the painful reality. Richard recognizes his own sins:

> And here have I the daintiness of ear
> To check time broke in a disorder'd string;
> But for the concord of my state and time
> Had not an ear to hear my true time broke:
> I wasted time, and now cloth time waste me.

(V.v.45ff.)

And this in turn is accompanied by a recognition of the vanity of a life lived without some transforming principle that takes the self beyond the self:

> Nor I, nor any man that but man is,
> With nothing shall be pleas'd, till he be eas'd
> With being nothing.

(V.v.39ff.)

The expected death comes abruptly—'How now! what means death in this rude assault?' Editors find this line perplexing, but the meaning is surely clear: death has not come in any of its fancifully imagined forms, it is simply brutal. In a sense the play ends with the heavily stressed monosyllabic line,

> thy fierce hand
> Hath with the king's blood stain'd the king's own land.

(V.v.109–10)

Those scenes of the last act from which Richard is absent, showing glimpses of the new world in which Bolingbroke rules, seem in some ways perfunctory and immature, and it is hard to take much interest in Aumerle's abortive conspiracy or the scene in which the Duchess of York pleads for her son's life. Sometimes the verse descends to doggerel, which may perhaps be, as Dover Wilson thinks, left over from an older play—though it is hard to see why Shakespeare should have let his attention lapse at just these points. It is indeed difficult to be sure of the reason for the unevenness of the last act, but certainly the poor verse of V.iii and V.vi makes the scene of the murder staid out in strong contrast—and this not only in an easy theatrical effectiveness. Bolingbroke exercises kingly power with more firmness than Richard had done, and he shows clemency to Aumerle; but—and there is a parallel here with the opening scenes of the play—behind the public exercise of kingly rights lies illegality, and an act so bad that it can only be hinted at. It seems at least possible that the explanation of the silly rhymes and the almost farcical note of parts of the Aumerle scenes is that all this is intended to emphasize the superficial character of authority divorced from the moral foundations of rule. The reality is murder:

> Riddles lie here, or in a word—
> Here lies blood.

As Traversi suggests, Bolingbroke's 'absorbing pursuit of power' is, in the nature of things, not likely to lay firmer foundations than Richard's abnegation of responsibility. The world of the unsuccessful egotist has collapsed; the nature of the world constructed by the realist politician, Henry IV, will be shown in the plays that bear his name.

The Personal Drama of Richard II

S.C. Sen Gupta

S.C. Sen Gupta argues that *Richard II* is better viewed as a human drama of a protagonist's fall than as a political or morality play. Gupta maintains that Shakespeare's interpretation of historical events makes Richard a Renaissance man responsible for his own fate; that is, Richard's cruelty, cowardice, and self-indulgent woe make Bolingbroke's takeover inevitable. S.C. Sen Gupta has been professor of English at Jadavpur University in Calcutta, India, and he has contributed numerous articles to professional journals.

Contradictory interpretations have been made—ever since the time of Shakespeare—of *Richard II,* which has been looked upon as both a plea for and a warning against rebellion. That Richard II was guilty of serious misgovernment is undoubted, but did he deserve to lose his crown? And even if he so deserved, had Bolingbroke the right to depose him, or had his subjects any right to try him? Various answers are given to these questions by various dramatic characters, and the most reasonable view is to take these answers as characteristic of the speakers—as, indeed, they almost always are—rather than as expositions of a particular view of history or politics. The principal commentators on men and events, besides the Bishop of Carlisle . . . are the King's uncles—Lancaster and York—and the philosophical Gardener. When we meet Gaunt in this play, he is no longer the formidable warrior of whom Falstaff speaks in *1 Henry IV;* he is old and dying, more a prophet inspired than a man of action. . . .

The King's other uncle, the Duke of York, is 'neuter' and may represent Shakespeare's views as much as Gaunt—and better. York first stands for the principle of order or 'degree', which critics look upon as the basic theme of Shakespeare's historical plays. After Gaunt's death, he stands for Hereford's rights, because Hereford may come to possess his father's properties by the accepted law of succession. . . .

THE SIGNIFICANCE OF THE GARDENER'S SCENE

If there is any scene in the play which may be regarded as symbolically suggestive, it is the one in which the Gardener and his servant moralize on their commonwealth. The Gardener is equally hard on

> too fast growing sprays,
> That look too lofty in our commonwealth,
>
> (III.iv.34–35)

and on

> The noisome weeds that without profit suck
> The soil's fertility from wholesome flowers.
>
> (III.iv.38–39)

The noisome weeds are Wiltshire, Bushy, and Green, but is not Bolingbroke a too fast growing spray that disturbs the peace of the commonwealth? The best way to interpret this scene would be to ignore its political overtones and emphasize only its dramatic significance. The comments made by Gaunt and York are characteristic of old men who are supposed to have authority but are powerless to act. The Gardener is a representative of the common men who had cooled towards Richard and whose attitude is graphically described later on by the Duke of York:

> As in a theatre, the eyes of men,
> After a well-grac'd actor leaves the stage,
> Are idly bent on him that enters next,
> Thinking his prattle to be tedious;
> Even so, or with much more contempt, men's eyes
> Did scowl on Richard: no man cried, 'God save him';
>
> (V.ii.23–28)

The Gardener is too refined and contemplative to be classed with those barbarians whose 'rude misgovern'd hands' threw dust and rubbish on King Richard's head, but he expresses their point of view, speaking 'no more than every one doth know'. Richard allowed noisome weeds to suck the soil's fertility from wholesome flowers, and no wonder if

> He that hath suffer'd this disorder'd spring
> Hath now himself met with the fall of leaf;
>
> (III.iv.48–49)

Not that the Gardener is an exponent of the philosophy of rebellion any more than of order; he only accepts the change from 'plume-pluck'd Richard' to mighty Bolingbroke as inevitable.

THE HUMAN DRAMA OF RICHARD'S FALL

Richard II is best read as a human drama rather than as a political document or as a moral homily. It is a personal tragedy like *Richard III,* that is to say, the emphasis is more on the declining fortunes of a single protagonist than on the course of events, or the social picture, or the development of any idea. Although the play deals with the reign of Richard II, there is no mention of the Peasants' Revolt or of Wyclif and the Lollards. There are critics who think that the tragic denouement in this play is 'explicable only through the action of Fortune's sightless wheel, in whose motion consisted the medieval idea of tragedy'. But by making Richard personally responsible for his disasters, Shakespeare seems to stress his independence of the medieval idea of tragedy and show in the true Renaissance spirit that man is the architect of his fate and not a victim of the blind goddess Fortune. Even in the opening scene, Bolingbroke, in defying Mowbray really accuses Richard of shedding the blood of a near kinsman:

> Which blood, like sacrificing Abel's cries
> Even from the tongueless caverns of the earth,
> To me for justice and rough chastisement;
> And, by the glorious worth of my descent
> This arm shall do it, or this life be spent.
>
> (I.i.104–08)

Abel was murdered by his brother Cain, and everyone could see who played Cain's part here. Mowbray's defence is vague but it further incriminates Richard:

> For Gloucester's death,
> I slew him not; but to mine own disgrace
> Neglected my sworn duty in that case,
>
> (I.i.132–34))

thus showing that whoever murdered Gloucester, the directive came from the King. In this scene, it is not merely his criminality that is brought to light but also his weakness, his powerlessness to command the militant lords to silence. When we meet him next at the lists[1] at Coventry, a medieval

---

1. combat ground enclosed by a fortification

tournament is described in all its elaborate detail. But what is dramatically significant is that it is utterly unnecessary, for Richard and his Councillors decide that the combat must not take place. The scene shows that he enjoys a dramatic situation as an end in itself and must have relished his own somewhat piquant role—he can banish but not 'atone' the contestants—in it.

Richard has observed the tremendous farewell given by the common people to Bolingbroke, and himself says, rather prophetically, that it seemed that the whole of England were in reversion Bolingbroke's. But, strangely enough, he allows himself to be persuaded that he need not worry about Bolingbroke and proceeds to confiscate Gaunt's property. He is both a bully and a coward. When there are powerful people before him, he cowers and cannot face a critical situation, but he is churlishly arrogant to a dying uncle and has no scruple about seizing what belongs to a man whom he has himself exiled and whose popularity he has observed.

When he returns from Ireland, there is a sea-change in his attitude to life, of which the only hint he had earlier was his love for theatrical shows. The rash young man who acted arrogantly and sometimes treacherously, has now become a poetical dawdler. Shakespeare follows history faithfully, reproducing the different stages of Richard's downfall—the conspiracy at home and abroad, the disloyalty of the peers who weighed the scales in favour of Bolingbroke, the desertion of the Welsh troops, the hostility of the common people, the march to London, the trial and the deposition. But he completely transforms the chronicle narrative by placing at the centre of the action—or inaction—a dreamer who gives away a kingdom in order to be able to luxuriate in his griefs. In vain does Carlisle, the best of his supporters, urge him to rally his forces and meet the enemy. He now sees himself in a new light and is content to contemplate his own downfall. He was a believer in the divine right of kings, which no subject could touch. If that magic will not work, he is no more than a man and has no right to call himself a king:

> throw away respect,
> Tradition, form, and ceremonious duty,
> For you have mistook me all this while:
> I live with bread like you, feel want,
> Taste grief, need friends: subjected thus,
> How can you say to me I am a king?

(III.ii.172–7)

How this poetical fantast lay concealed behind the arrogant wastrel of the first two acts has not been represented in course of the action. That is the only thing 'enigmatic' about Richard's character, and the greatest defect of the drama *as* drama. But it is this trait in his character, a pure invention of Shakespeare, which explains his catastrophic end. [Victorian essayist Charles] Lamb speaks of the reluctant pangs of abdicating Royalty, but are the pangs entirely 'reluctant'? Rather it seems that his griefs are a commodity which pleases as much as it galls him. When he says to the usurping Bolingbroke:

> I thank thee, king,
> For thy great bounty, that not only giv'st
> Me cause to wail, but teachest me the way
> How to lament the cause,
>
> (IV.i.299–302)

he is not entirely ironical.

RICHARD ACCEDES TO BOLINGBROKE

In Holinshed, Northumberland is sent by Bolingbroke to the King at Conway, and the King is brought to Flint Castle, virtually a prisoner. After this he is held fast in the mighty hold of Bolingbroke; and the reception accorded by the people, as the two potentates journey to London, makes it clear that the deposition, which comes off without delay, will be a mere formality. Indeed, the feeling against Richard is so strong that if he were not committed to the Tower, worse things might happen:[2]

> 'Manie evill disposed persons, assembling themselves together in great numbers, intended to have met with him, and to have taken him from such as had the conveieng of him, that they might have slaine him. But the mayor and aldermen gathered to them the worshipfull commoners and grave citizens, by whose policie, and not without much adoo, the other were revoked from their evill purpose.'

By means of slight changes here and there, Shakespeare transforms the above episode and makes Richard primarily responsible for his deposition. Although he has received some rude shocks—the departure of the Welsh army, the beheading of his favourites by Bolingbroke who has repealed himself—his cause is not irretrievably lost, and both Carlisle and Aumerle in Flint Castle think that he may yet consoli-

2. according to Holinshed in *Chronicles II*

date his forces. But even before Richard comes to Flint Castle, he describes himself as the slave of woe, and when he
meets Bolingbroke at the base court of the Castle,

> Sorrow and grief of heart
> Makes him speak fondly, like a frantic man:

> (III.iii.184–5)

No wonder that although Bolingbroke at this stage claims
only his Lancastrian possessions and Richard has no idea of
what the London mob will do, he speaks of deposing himself
and refers to his cousin as King Bolingbroke. In Holinshed's
narrative, although the King is more or less a prisoner, at
Flint Castle he promises no more than that the Duke will
enjoy all that is his, without exception. But Shakespeare's
Richard makes a characteristic addition:

> Your own is yours, and I am yours, and all.

> (III.iii.197)

Yet another interesting modification is that whereas in the
chronicle narratives charges are first preferred and considered in Parliament and then the King is persuaded to resign,
in Shakespeare's play Bolingbroke is busy investigating in
Westminster Hall the murder of his uncle the Duke of
Gloucester when he is interrupted by the following an-
nouncement made by the Duke of York:

> Great Duke of Lancaster, I come to thee
> From plume-pluck'd Richard; who with willing soul
> Adopts thee heir, and his high sceptre yields
> To the possession of thy royal hand.

> (IV.i.107–10)

And Bolingbroke answers:

> In God's name, I'll ascend the regal throne.

> (IV.i.113)

It is only after this that Richard is fetched to Parliament House

> that in common view
> He may surrender;

> (IV.i.155–6)

and the importance of the reception by Londoners is so
much minimized that it is only later reported by the Duke of
York to his Duchess.

BOLINGBROKE'S MOTIVE FOR DEPOSING RICHARD

The question has very often been debated whether Bolingbroke's seizure of the throne was the climax of a carefully
planned campaign, or whether he only accepted a 'rever-

sion' he did not originally aim at. In the sources—in Holinshed as well as in Froissart[3]—Bolingbroke was promised assistance by the nobility as well as the prelacy[4] 'if he expelling King Richard, as a man not meet for the office he bare, would take upon him the scepter, rule and diademe of his native land and religion'. The poet Samuel Daniel, too, says that he at first proceeded warily seeming not to affect that which he did effect. Shakespeare omits all such suggestions, and in view of the fact that he has based his play on Holinshed and Froissart and might have been acquainted with Daniel's poem, the omission seems to be deliberate. 'Was Shakespeare', says R.F. Hill, 'trying to show Bolingbroke, as Dover Wilson puts it, as "borne upward by a power beyond his volition", or was the suppression designed to achieve the ambiguity of a politic usurper? All the clues point to the second alternative'. But there may be a third alternative which does not exclude the first two and shows them to be not indeed incompatible. Bolingbroke—whatever his supporters in the chronicles might have thought—does return in the play only to claim his patrimony, but he is a normally ambitious man and behaves as such a man might be expected to behave. He thinks of the murder of Richard only after the Oxford conspiracy makes him realize how dangerous a living deposed king might be for his successor. Such a thought would not, of course, come to a really pious man, but Bolingbroke is too worldly-minded to be really pious. It is also characteristic of him that after the murder of Richard, he asks for God's pardon for this woeful act, but he does not think that there was anything illegal or immoral about his assumption of royalty. He has, however, a very unquiet time as king, and finds that even if the deposition of Richard was justified, he has little to say to those who make out a case for Edmund Mortimer, Earl of March. *Henry VI* has more than one reference to the Mortimer claim, and one of the reasons why the Percies raise the standard of rebellion in *Henry IV* is that the Earl of March—Shakespeare, following Holinshed, makes a confusion between the uncle and the nephew—has a better title to the throne than Bolingbroke. It is significant that there is not the faintest reference to this subject in *Richard II,* where even the Bishop of Carlisle, Bolingbroke's most unsparing critic, does not advance any plea on behalf

3. *The Ancient Chronicles of Sir John Froissart*   4. high-ranking members of the clergy

RICHARD CONTEMPLATES HIS DOWNFALL

In act 3, scene 3, Richard speaks of himself in third person as he anticipates his fall. Shakespeare portrays him as a spineless king who, fearing Bolingbroke, indulges in grief and defeatism.

RICHARD. What must the King do now? Must he submit?
  The King shall do it. Must he be deposed?
  The King shall be contented. Must he lose
  The name of king? a[1] God's name, let it go.
  I'll give my jewels for a set of beads;[2]
  My gorgeous palace for a hermitage;
  My gay apparel for an almsman's gown;
  My figured[3] goblets for a dish of wood;
  My scepter for a palmer's[4] walking-staff;
  My subjects for a pair of carved saints;
  And my large kingdom for a little grave,
  A little, little grave, an obscure grave;
  Or I'll be buried in the King's highway,
  Some way of common trade,[5] where subjects' feet
  May hourly trample on their sovereign's head;
  For on my heart they tread now whilst I live,
  And buried once, why not upon my head?
  Aumerle, thou weep'st, my tender-hearted cousin:
  We'll make foul weather with despised tears;
  Our sighs and they shall lodge[6] the summer corn,
  And make a dearth in this revolting land:
  Or shall we play the wantons[7] with our woes
  And make some pretty match with shedding tears,
  As thus, to drop them still[8] upon one place,
  Till they have fretted[9] us a pair of graves
  Within the earth; and, therein laid, "there lies
  Two kinsmen digged their graves with weeping eyes":
  Would not this ill do well? Well, well, I see
  I talk but idly, and you laugh at me.
  Most mighty prince, my Lord Northumberland,
  What says King Bolingbroke? Will his Majesty
  Give Richard leave to live till Richard die?
  You make a leg,[10] and Bolingbroke says "Ay."

1. *a* in   2. *set of beads* rosary   3. *figured* ornamented   4. *palmer's* pilgrims
5. *trade* coming and going   6. *lodge* beat down   7. *play the wantons* be
unrestrained   8. *still* always   9. *fretted* worn   10. *make a leg* curtsy

of the line of the Duke of Clarence. It is evident that in *Richard II,* Bolingbroke has no scruples of conscience about gaining the crown, for his ambition and the occasion fit into each other, and considerations to be urged afterwards are not mentioned at all. When later he speaks of the by-paths and indirect, crooked ways by means of which he wormed his way to the throne, he has the same kind of hindsight that Hamlet displays when he exclaims before the Ghost:

> O my prophetic soul!
> My uncle!
>
> (*Hamlet*, I.v.40–41)

Or it is like the illumination that comes, more dramatically, to Emilia, when after the exposure of Iago's conspiracy, she is at first puzzled and then exclaims:

> Villany! villany! villany!
> I think upon's, I think, I smell't; O villany!
> I thought so then, I'll kill myself for grief.
>
> (*Othello*, V.ii.188–90)

Departing from Hall's view of Henry IV as the first author of the civil strife that later on raged in England, Shakespeare presents him in this play as a man who seizes the crown but is no usurper because his ambition grows with his opportunities and the crown is to him more a gift than a prize won by force or diplomacy.

Historical plays deal not with one action but with periods of time covering a multiplicity of incidents. Such periods may—as in *Henry V*—be given an effective unity through the reigning monarch who is supposed to be connected with all that happens during his time. Still drama is not history and requires greater concentration than is found in a chronicle of events. That is why the playwright focuses attention on one important action, presented as the central theme of a long reign. Such is the deposition of Richard in *Richard II*.

The Character of Richard III

H.M. Richmond

H.M. Richmond argues that Richard III is a genius whose power and charm propel him to diabolical acts. As his talents lead others to self-destruction, the audience too succumbs to Richard's wit and egoism until finally his cruelty appears repulsive and self-destructive. Richmond maintains that Richard's larger-than-life character is better suited for a medieval morality play illustrating evil than for a history play regarding the uncertainties of political activities. H.M. Richmond has taught at the University of California at Berkeley, where he specialized in Renaissance English literature. He is the author of *The School of Love: The Evolution of the Stuart Love Lyric.*

The character of Richard himself is obviously central to [Shakespeare's] achievement, which to a large extent is the result of the simple fact that Richard *is* central. From Richard's opening "aria," we are left in no doubt where the focus of interest will lie, and whose point of view will color our view of the action. Edward may still be king at the start of the play and, at the end, the Tudors may supplant Richard; yet his career remains the dominant theme throughout. . . .

RICHARD IS A PSYCHOLOGICALLY MODERN CHARACTER

Richard remains for most of us an extremely modern character, one that lends itself to modern psychological analysis both in terms of the character himself, and in his relation to the audience. The issue of Richard's deformity (of which there is no trace in the realistic portrait of the historical Richard in the National Portrait Gallery) is a fashionable theme of psychological debate. Shakespeare, wisely alert to

From *Shakespeare's Political Plays*, by H.M. Richmond (New York: Random House, 1967). Reprinted by permission of the author.

the need for at least a surface plausibility of motivation, uses several soliloquies to make Richard's deformity the key to his compensatory ruthlessness. He shows the understandable hostility of the cripple for his more happily endowed contemporaries:

> But I, that am curtail'd[1] of this fair proportion,[2]
> Cheated of feature by dissembling[3] nature,
> Deform'd, unfinish'd, sent before my time
> Into this breathing world, scarce half made up,
> And that so lamely and unfashionable
> That dogs bark at me as I halt[4] by them;
> Why, I, in this weak piping time[5] of peace,
> Have no delight to pass away the time,
> Unless to spy my shadow in the sun
> And descant[6] on my own deformity:
> And therefore, since I cannot prove a lover,
> To entertain[7] these fair well-spoken days,
> I am determined to prove a villain.

(I.i.18–30)

Yet if we consider the logic of other characters in the play, this self-interpretation is the merest rationalization. Far from being the cause of Richard's villainy, his deformity would, to many medieval and renaissance minds, be the symptom of it—like the devil's cloven hoof and his other bestial trappings. . . . He appears from his birth to be a more or less diabolical personality. That is his power—and his charm.

RICHARD IS A POWERFUL AND CHARMING CHARACTER

For Richard surpasses any earlier Shakespearean character in hypnotic power. To a large extent, this arises from his capacity both to grasp fully his own evil nature, and to act in accordance with it, untrammeled by such hesitations and regrets as beset a character like Macbeth. Yet Richard's cheerful and efficient villainy, far from repelling the audience, delights it. This confidence in the audience's response shows Shakespeare's power to break through the crust of rationalizing moral prejudice and respect for decorum to the disruptive inner springs of human motivation. Richard has the fascination of the superman—intelligent, witty, superior to human limitations and virtues. More seriously, he is the focus for the vicarious release of all the repressed resentments and desires that men share in a complex, organized

1. *curtailed* cut short   2. *proportion* shape   3. *dissembling* cheating   4. *halt* limp
5. *piping time* when shepherds play their pipes   6. *descant* warble   7. *entertain* pass away

society—and which we have seen disastrously liberated in the English aristocrats of Shakespeare's earlier studies of the Wars of the Roses. . . .

Above all we sympathize with Richard's contempt for cant and superstition, triumphantly illustrated by his refusal to be discountenanced by the lack of sunshine before his last battle:

> Not shine today! Why what is that to me
> More than to Richmond? for the selfsame heaven
> That frowns on me looks sadly upon him.

(V.iii.285–7)

Richard's ability to rise above the necessities of compromise must fascinate all those who feel the burden of apparently inescapable decorum and constraint that civilization imposes on our basic instincts. . . .

Yet if a work of art is to be more than a sociological phenomenon, it must have some motivating principle that is superior to providing vicarious satisfaction for primitive impulses. In fact, one may wonder whether the character of Richard is not given false prominence because of the almost pathological excitement he arouses. It might be considered a serious criticism of Richard as a character in a history play to say that not only is he a gross misrepresentation of an historical person who was no worse (and possibly even a little better) than his contemporaries, but also that his personality is completely incredible. . . .

THE MEDIEVAL NOTION OF SYMBOLIC GOOD AND EVIL

If anything, the other characters see their world more clearly than does Richard as the medieval one into which both metaphysical evil and metaphysical good enter freely and intelligibly.

This view is conspicuously characteristic of Queen Margaret, whose unpredictable but plausible transmutation from ambitious sentimentalist to avenging angel is one of the most brilliant strokes of character development in Shakespeare. Margaret haunts the action of *Richard III*, her rhetorical vehemence and utter acceptance of the medieval cosmic order making her a worthy spiritual antagonist of Richard. To her question:

> Can curses pierce the clouds and enter heaven?

(I.iii.195)

she later makes her own emphatic reply:

I'll not believe but they ascend the sky,
And there awake God's gentle-sleeping peace.

(I.iii.287–8)

Even Richard seems somewhat intimidated by the volcanic prophecies she launches at him and attempts to turn them aside by a trick. . . .

He and Margaret are the two poles between which the body of the play revolves, and her estimate of his nature remains the most valuable in the play. If she is an avenging angel in intent, he is God's scourge of man's villainy in practice. As Margaret perceives:

Richard yet lives, hell's black intelligencer,
Only reserved their factor, to buy souls
And send them thither.

(IV.iv.71–3)

Richard functions, for her, as an agent of the Devil—buying up lost souls, and sending them to hell; and this is no idle conceit of a lunatic mind. . . .

THE SIGNIFICANCE OF CHARACTERS THAT RICHARD AFFECTS

And since a diabolical spirit is inflexible by nature and cannot properly be the essential subject of drama (any more than Satan can be the hero of *Paradise Lost*), it becomes necessary to reshape our view of the play, in order to see that the real evolution of dynamic action lies outside Richard. It lies in the minds of the English men and women whom he appears to betray. . . .

If we see Richard as a catalyst, or better still as a reflection, of the latent will and the greedy self-deception of those with whom he has dealings, many curious scenes become more meaningful. Perhaps the most conspicuous of these is the extraordinary second scene of the play in which Richard manages to win the favor of the woman whose husband he has murdered. Lady Anne is a somewhat conventional young woman, as her stilted laments over the bier of Henry VI reveal—they are full of parallelisms, repetitions and extravagance. Into this solemn rhythm Richard breaks brusquely, like an unchaste thought; and Lady Anne identifies him melodramatically, yet with unconscious exactness, as a "minister of hell," a "foul devil." She soon finds this very flamboyance of hers a weakness, since it allows her opponent to strike a plausible attitude of moderation and suave religiosity once his energy has broken through her endless lament. Richard shows all the skill of the virtuoso in excuses such as modern psychiatry ascribes to the rationalizations of pathological desires. His very effrontery and sophistication blunt opposition, once one deigns to argue with him on the same plane. . . .

For all her curses Anne cannot, in this context of emotional confusion, find the authority to act as decisively as she has spoken. More moderation earlier would have made such a challenge meaningless now, but once she has admitted her earlier extravagance, Richard forces her back relentlessly, even offering to kill himself now if she asks it. . . . Yet Anne's deception by Richard is not merely episodic; it is the norm for all but the most hardened judges (like Margaret) in the play. Most seriously of all, it is the norm for the readers and audience also.

The *coup de théàtre*[8] by which Richard wins Anne establishes us also as his victims, for if intellectually we see a little deeper into him than she does, we are still prone to view his victims from his own merciless perspective, at least unconsciously. We laugh at his macabre jokes and connive in his plots by enjoying his sardonic asides and soliloquies. There is surely also a poetic truth in Richard's seduction of Anne that is related to her historical nature: she must have married the real Richard at least in part from the desire to find any plausible refuge from the anarchy of the times. . . .

Whatever its roots in history, this second scene of the play establishes the rhetorical seductiveness by which evil insinuates itself—if anything more easily into the hearts of those who are to be most afflicted by its consequences. And the play takes its course through the exposition and evaluation of those states of mind in which evil is conceived, accepted, and expiated. This, rather than any logical historical process, governs the sequence of events in the plot. Anne's reversal of feeling is followed first by the contrasting rigor of Margaret's denunciation of Richard, and then by a detailed study, in Clarence's nightmare sequence in the Tower, of the fate of those like Anne and Clarence, who switch allegiances on the selfish impulse of the moment. . . .

Failure in discrimination is a uniform characteristic of all Richard's victims. Rivers earlier had praised Richard's moderation in his censure of Clarence's murderers, not realizing

8. dramatic turn of events

that Richard was carefully taking into account his own part in the assassination.

This kind of lucidity on Richard's part is another super-human characteristic of his mind; it stands in interesting contrast to the apparently analogous character of Bucking-ham, who is the most sustained conventional character study in the play.... The relationship with Buckingham in its early phases well illustrates the essentially catalytic role that Richard usually plays whenever he impinges on the moral responsibility of others. He has power over the bodies of those around him, but not over their wills; it is with their own assent that he destroys them morally, allowing their weaknesses scope rather than enforcing his own personality upon them. Buckingham is quite indignant at the idea that Richard would need to teach him duplicity....

Hitherto, not unlike the audience, Buckingham has en-joyed Richard's wit, and taken advantage of the political fi-nesse it fosters; at this point, however, neither Buckingham nor the audience can find any delight in such a massacre of innocents—an act of diabolical rather than human propor-tions. There is weight in the severing of relations by Richard:

> The deep-revolving witty Buckingham
> No more shall be the neighbour to my counsel:
> Hath he so long held out with me untired,
> And stops he now for breath?

> (IV.ii.42–5)

However, Richard's momentum is like that of human am-bition—it flags when the goal is reached, in this case the Crown of England. Thereafter, Buckingham's departure marks the conclusion of one major phase of Richard's role as epitome of the magnetic, dark passion of egotism. From about this point on, Shakespeare concerns himself with the negative, declining aspects of this element of Richard's per-sonality. Richard is essentially an abstract of certain human traits; in that sense, the logic of his fall is only superficially naturalistic. In the earlier parts of the play, Shakespeare has chosen to show the ruthless efficiency of egotism. To give the sequence harmony with the overall rhythm of the Wheel of Fortune in the second part he illustrates the negative phases of egotism, its self-destructive character. In the scene before Buckingham's instinctive revulsion, Lady Anne gives a firm indication of the subconscious penalties that are as-sociated with Richard's conscious virtuosity, whose demands undermine his inward stability:

> For never yet one hour in his bed
> Have I enjoyed the golden dew of sleep,
> But have been waked by his timorous dreams.

(IV.i.83–5)

RICHARD LOSES CHARM AND BECOMES REPULSIVE

In harmony with this revelation, the scene immediately following Buckingham's revulsion starts with Tyrrel's pathetic
description of the murder of Richard's innocent victims in
the Tower—a description carefully calculated to alienate the
audience's sympathy from Richard, and to lessen their delight in his wit, which is thereafter no longer allowed the
same virtuosity. His wife's death is revealed with parenthetic
and humorless casualness:

> And Anne my wife hath bid the world good night.

(IV.iii.39)

and the next scene gathers a symbolic triad of affronted
women: Queen Margaret, Queen Elizabeth, and the Duchess
of York. . . .

Richard's confrontation by his mother and Queen Elizabeth sets the seal on his downward course. His mother's
powerful curse is followed by the attempt to win Queen Elizabeth's daughter, a scene as joyless as the earlier courtship
of Anne was vivacious and dashing. Not only does Elizabeth
fail to live up to Richard's expectations, but his loss of enthusiasm and poise causes him soon after to chide Catesby
for not leaving with a message that Richard has actually for-
gotten to give him, and later Richard becomes so upset by
bad news that he even strikes the innocent bearer of the
news. Just before the battle Richard asks for wine to revive
his jaded spirit, confessing:

> I have not that alacrity of spirit,
> Nor cheer of mind, that I was wont to have.

(V.iii.73–4)

This loss of energy is not shown in terms of Richard's conscience, as with Macbeth's, but externally, as if by metaphysical requirement. Richard's dream epitomizes this
sense of an external, fated rhythm in the play. The victims of
Richard are massed ritually in a counterpoint of curses on
Richard and blessings on Richmond. . . .

Despite the sequence of vignettes of human fallibility,
Richard III progresses conceptually and dogmatically, not

psychologically and pragmatically. Perhaps the strongest illustration of this lies in Richard's extraordinary speech when he wakes from his nightmare. There is no passion in Richard's self-analysis, merely paradoxical rhetoric:

> What do I fear? myself? there's none else by:
> Richard loves Richard; that is, I am I.
> Is there a murderer here? No. Yes, I am.
> Then fly. What, from myself? Great reason why:
> Lest I revenge. What, myself upon myself?
> Alack, I love myself. Wherefore? for any good
> That I myself have done unto myself?
> O, no! alas, I rather hate myself
> For hateful deeds committed by myself.
>
> (V.iii.182–90)

He coldly determines that even he finds "in myself no pity to myself." A more analytic estimate of the situation could hardly have been provided by a medieval theologian.

If then *Richard III* is a triumph dramatically through its humorous, Machiavellian villain-hero, its achievements are nevertheless not those of the history play. It derives from and returns to the world of myth: the larger-than-life whose functions are schematic, not compromised by the ambiguities and confusions that are near the heart of all political activity.

Richard III Is a Religious Play

E.M.W. Tillyard

E.M.W. Tillyard argues that in *Richard III* Shakespeare portrays the restoration of England's political order as a religious event, in which the inevitable outcome shows the hand of God. Tillyard shows that Richard's diabolical behavior brings previously opposing forces together to overcome him, thus enacting a larger moral scheme. E.M.W. Tillyard taught at Jesus College, Cambridge University, in England. He is the author of *Poetry Direct and Oblique*, *The English Epic and Its Background*, and *The English Renaissance: Fact or Fiction?*

In spite of the eminence of Richard's character the main business of [*Richard III*] is to complete the national tetralogy[1] and to display the working out of God's plan to restore England to prosperity. . . .

Both *1 Henry VI* and *Richard III*, unlike the other plays, have a clear-marked hero, and both heroes have a Frenchwoman as their chief opponent. Talbot stands for order and Richard for its contrary, chaos, and whereas Joan prospers in her efforts to humiliate England, Margaret through her curses unwittingly creates the unity of the land she has so terribly injured. Again, in *1 Henry VI* the nobles are wantonly disunited, while in *Richard III* they are schooled by their sufferings into a unity otherwise unattainable. When there is already so much evidence that Shakespeare wrote his tetralogy deliberately and academically and that he was deeply influenced by the Morality tradition with its medieval passion for equivalences, it is not pressing things to assert

---

1. consisting of *1*, *2*, and *3 Henry VI* and *Richard III*

From *Shakespeare's History Plays*, by E.M.W. Tillyard (London: Chatto & Windus, 1946). Reprinted by permission from the Estate of E.M.W. Tillyard and the publisher.

that Shakespeare fully intended the above cross-references between the first and last plays of his series.

THE POLITICAL THEME OF RESTORING ORDER

However, the greatest bond uniting all four plays is the steady political theme: the theme of order and chaos, of proper political degree and civil war, of crime and punishment, of God's mercy finally tempering his justice, of the belief that such had been God's way with England.

I noticed that in each part of *Henry VI* there was some positive, usually very formal or stylised reference to the principle of order. In *1 Henry VI* there was the scene of Talbot doing homage to his king, in *2 Henry VI* the blameless conduct of Iden and his perfect contentment with his own station in life, in *3 Henry VI* Henry's pathetic longing for the precisely ordered life of a shepherd. In *Richard III* Shakespeare both continues this technique by inserting the choric scene of the three citizens ... and at the end of the play comes out with his full declaration of the principle of order, thus giving final and unmistakable shape to what, though largely implicit, had been all along the animating principle of the tetralogy. His instrument, obviously and inevitably, is Richmond; and that this instrument should be largely passive, truly an instrument (hence likely to be overlooked or made little of by the modern reader) was also inevitable in the sort of drama Shakespeare was writing. In the tremendous evolution of God's plans the accidents of character must not be obtruded.[2] Every sentence of Richmond's last speech, today regarded as a competent piece of formality, would have raised the Elizabethans to an ecstasy of feeling. Richmond gets everything right and refers to all the things they minded about. ...

RELIGIOUS ELEMENTS IN THE PLAY

And if one were to say that in *Richard III* Shakespeare pictures England restored to order through God's grace, one gravely risks being lauded or execrated for attributing to Shakespeare personally the full doctrine of prevenient Grace according to Calvin.[3] When therefore I say that *Richard III is* a very religious play, I want to be understood as speaking of

2. imposed on others; pushed forward   3. Swiss theologian John Calvin preached the doctrine that God's chosen were saved by God's grace alone.

the play and not of Shakespeare. For the purposes of the tetralogy and most obviously for this play Shakespeare accepted the prevalent belief that God had guided England into her haven of Tudor prosperity. And he had accepted it with his whole heart. . . . In the same spirit Shakespeare drops hints of a divine purpose in the mass of vengeance that forms the substance of the play, of a direction in the seemingly endless concatenation of crime and punishment.[4] . . .

But the full religious temper of the play only comes out in the two great scenes in the last third of the play: the lamentations of the three queens after Richard has murdered the princes in the Tower, and the ghosts appearing to Richard and Richmond before Bosworth. These are both extreme and splendid examples of the formal style which I suggested above [and] should be considered the norm rather than the exception in the tetralogy. Both scenes are ritual and incantatory to a high degree, suggesting an ecclesiastical context; both are implicitly or explicitly pious; and both are archaic, suggesting the prevalent piety of the Middle Ages. . . .

RICHARD'S IMPORTANCE IN THE POLITICAL AND RELIGIOUS SCHEME

That the play's main end is to show the working out of God's will in English history does not detract from the importance of Richard in the process and from his dominance as a character. And it is through his dominance that he is able to be the instrument of God's ends. Whereas the sins of other men had merely bred more sins, Richard's are so vast that they are absorptive, not contagious. He is the great ulcer of the body politic into which all its impurity is drained and against which all the members of the body politic are united. It is no longer a case of limb fighting limb but of the war of the whole organism against an ill which has now ceased to be organic. The metaphor of poison is constantly applied to Richard, and that of beast, as if here were something to be excluded from the human norm. Queen Margaret unites the two metaphors when she calls him "that poisonous bunchback'd toad" and that "bottled spider," the spider being proverbially venomous.

In making Richard thus subservient to a greater scheme I do not deny that for many years now the main attraction of

4. crime and punishment interconnected as are links in a chain

the play has actually been Richard's character in itself. . . .

A number of people have written well on the character of Richard: in one place or another all has been said that need be said. It remains now to think less in terms of alternatives and to include more than is usually done in Richard's character, even at the sacrifice of consistency. Lamb, for instance, who in his brief references raised most of the pertinent questions, wants to exclude the melodramatic side:

> Shakespeare has not made Richard so black a monster as is supposed. Wherever he is monstrous, it was to conform to vulgar opinion. But he is generally a Man.

Actually Shakespeare was already at one with vulgar opinion and willingly makes him a monster. But only in some places; in others he keeps him human. Similarly we need not choose between Richard the psychological study in compensation for physical disability and Richard the embodiment of sheer demonic will, for he is both. It *is* true that, as Lamb notes, Richard in the allusions to his deformity

> mingles . . . a perpetual reference to his own powers and capacities, by which he is enabled to surmount these petty objections; and the joy of a defect *conquered,* or *turned* into an advantage, is one cause of these very allusions, and of the satisfaction, with which his mind recurs to them.

But [critic Edward] Dowden also is right when he says of Richard that

> his dominant characteristic is not intellectual; it is rather a daemonic energy of will. . . . He is of the diabolical class. . . . He is single-hearted in his devotion to evil. . . . He has a fierce joy, and he is an intense believer,—in the creed of hell. And therefore he is strong. He inverts the moral order of things, and tries to live in this inverted system. He does not succeed; he dashes himself to pieces against the laws of the world which he has outraged.

It might be retorted that the above distinction is superfluous, because an extreme manifestation of demonic will can only arise from the additional drive set in motion by an unusual need to compensate for a defect. But the point is that Shakespeare does actually make the distinction and that Richard, within the limits of the play, is psychologically both possible and impossible. He ranges from credibly motivated villain to a symbol, psychologically absurd however useful dramatically, of the diabolic.

This shift, however, is not irregular. In the first two scenes, containing his opening soliloquy, his dealings with

PEACE AND UNITY

In the final speech of Richard III, *Richmond reviews past animosities between the houses of York and Lancaster, welcomes the peace that follows Richard's defeat, and asks God's blessing on a new united England.*

RICHMOND. What men of name[1] are slain on either side?
STANLEY. John Duke of Norfolk, Walter Lord Ferrers,
Sir Robert Brakenbury, and Sir William Brandon.
RICHMOND. Inter their bodies as becomes their births:
Proclaim a pardon to the soldiers fled
That in submission will return to us:
And then, as we have ta'en the sacrament,
We will unite the white rose and the red.[2]
Smile heaven upon this fair conjunction,
That long have frowned upon their enmity!
What traitor hears me, and says not Amen?
England hath long been mad, and scarred herself;
The brother blindly shed the brother's blood,
The father rashly slaughtered his own son,
The son, compelled, been butcher to the sire:
All that divided York and Lancaster
Divided in their dire division,
O, now let Richmond and Elizabeth,
The true succeeders of each royal house,
By God's fair ordinance conjoin together!
And let their heirs, God if his will be so,
Enrich the time to come with smooth-faced peace,
With smiling plenty and fair prosperous days!
Abate the edge of traitors, gracious Lord,
That would reduce[3] these bloody days again,
And make poor England weep in streams of blood!
Let them not live to taste this land's increase
That would with treason wound this fair land's peace!
Now civil wounds are stopped, Peace lives again:
That she may long live here, God say Amen!

1. *name* high rank   2. *We . . . red* The two warring houses of York (white rose) and Lancaster (red rose) united when Richmond, as Henry VII, married Elizabeth, daughter of Edward IV.   3. *reduce* bring back

Clarence, his interruption of the funeral of Henry VI with his courtship of Ann Nevil, he is predominantly the psychological study. Shakespeare here builds up his private character. And he is credible; with his humour, his irony, and his artistry in crime acting as differentiating agents, creating a sense of the individual. After this he carries his established private character into the public arena, where he is more than a match for anyone except Queen Margaret. Of her alone he is afraid; and her curse establishes, along with the psychologically probable picture just created, the competing and ultimately victorious picture of the monstrosity, the country's scapegoat, the vast impostume of the common-wealth. She makes him both a cosmic symbol, the "troubler of the poor world's peace," and sub-human, a "rooting hog," "the slave of nature and the son of hell." She calls on him the curse of insomnia, which later we find to have been fulfilled. Clearly this does not apply to the exulting ironic Richard: *he* must always have slept with infant tranquillity. Thus Margaret's curse is prospective, and though he continues to pile up the materials for the construction of his monstrosity, it is the credible Richard, glorying in his will and his success in compensating his disabilities, who persists till the end of the third act and the attainment of the throne. Thenceforward, apart from his outburst of energy in courting Queen Elizabeth for her daughter's hand, he melts from credible character into a combination of sheer melodrama villain and symbol of diabolism. His irony forsakes him; he is un-guarded not secretive in making his plans; he is no longer cool but confused in his energy, giving and retracting orders; he *really* does not sleep; and, when on the eve of Bosworth he calls for a bowl of wine because he has not "that alacrity of spirit nor cheer of mind that I was wont to have," he is the genuine ancestor of the villain in a nine-teenth century melodrama calling for whiskey when things look black. Then, with the ghosts and his awakening into his Judas-like monologue, psychological probability and melo-dramatic villainy alike melt into the symbol of sheer denial and diabolism. Nor does his momentary resurrection at Bosworth with his memorable shout for a horse destroy that abiding impression. . . .

Finally we must not forget that Richard is the vehicle of an orthodox doctrine about kingship. It was a terrible thing to fight the ruling monarch, and Richard had been crowned. However, he was so clearly both a usurper and a murderer that he had qualified as a tyrant; and against an authentic tyrant it was lawful to rebel. Richmond, addressing his army before Bosworth, makes the point absolutely clear:

> Richard except, those whom we fight against
> Had rather have us win than him they follow.

> For what is he they follow? truly, gentlemen,
> A bloody tyrant and a homicide;
> One rais'd in blood and one in blood establish'd;
> One that made means to come by what he hath
> And slaughter'd those that were the means to help him;
> One that hath ever been God's enemy.
> Then if you fight against God's enemy,
> God will in justice ward you as his soldiers;
> If you do sweat to put a tyrant down,
> You sleep in peace, the tyrant being slain.

And Derby, handing Henry the crown after the battle, calls it "this long-usurped royalty."

QUEEN MARGARET FUNCTIONS AS A UNIFYING ELEMENT

I have indicated in outline the course of the play: the emerging of unity from and through discord, the simultaneous change in Richard from accomplished villain to the despairing embodiment of evil. Shakespeare gives it coherence through the dominant and now scarcely human figure of Queen Margaret: the one character who appears in every play. Being thus a connecting thread, it is fitting that she give structural coherence to the crowning drama. As Richard's downfall goes back to her curse, so do the fates of most of the characters who perish in the play go back to her curses or prophecies in the same scene, I. 3. Nor are her curses mere explosions of personal spite; they agree with the tit-for-tat scheme of crime and punishment that has so far prevailed in the tetralogy. She begins by recalling York's curse on her at Wakefield for the cruelty of her party to Rutland and the penalty she has paid; and then enumerates the precisely balanced scheme of retribution appointed for the house of York:

> If not by war, by surfeit die your king,
> As ours by murder, to make him a king.
> Edward thy son, which now is Prince of Wales,
> For Edward my son, which was Prince of Wales,
> Die in his youth by like untimely violence.
> Thyself a queen, for me that was a queen,
> Outlive thy glory like my wretched self.

Curses on minor characters follow, but Richard, as befits, has a speech to himself. His peculiar curse is the gnawing of conscience, sleeplessness, and the mistake of taking friends for enemies and enemies for friends. I have spoken of the sleeplessness above, how it could not apply to the Richard of the first three acts. Similarly it is not till Bosworth that the curse of thinking his enemies friends comes true. We are meant to think of it when Richmond says in lines quoted above that "those whom we fight against had rather have us win than him they follow." The man with the best brain in the play ends by being the most pitifully deceived....

But it is worth recording that Margaret in her last lines before she goes out unconsciously forecasts the larger theme of the plays. Talking of Richard she says:

Let each of you be subject to his hate,
And he to yours, and all of you to God's.

Margaret does not realise that this grouping of Yorkists against Richard will unite them to the Lancastrians similarly opposed, and that the just vengeance of God had even then given way to his mercy.

CHAPTER 3

The Henry Plays

READINGS ON
THE HISTORIES

Falstaff the Clown in *1 Henry IV*

Bente A. Videbæk

Bente A. Videbæk identifies Falstaff in *1 Henry IV* as a brilliantly funny clown, and cites examples of Falstaff's humor. But Videbæk explains that Falstaff also functions to clarify Hal's character and with his mockery gives the audience a detached view of serious historical events. Bente A. Videbæk, born in Denmark, earned degrees from the University of Copenhagen in Denmark and Northwestern University in Illinois. She is professor of English at Suffolk County Community College in New York.

Falstaff is the only Shakespearean clown character who has repeat performances. He appears in three of Shakespeare's plays and is mentioned in a fourth. Not everybody, however, will feel comfortable with the label of "clown" applied to him; indeed, Falstaff is often rather a genuine character than a clown, and at times the two aspects merge totally. . . . The historical Prince Hal may have been wild, but there is no reference to a historical person like the Shakespearean Falstaff. Shakespeare creates him for *1 Henry IV* to fulfill a theatrical function, to give flesh and substance to the escapades of Prince Hal so Hal himself remains largely unblemished and may ascend the throne with unstained character. . . .

The two parts of *Henry IV* retell one aspect of the historical facts of the reign of the usurper. King Henry IV is a troubled human being, who is constantly thwarted by both external and internal circumstances; but though the two plays bear his name, they serve chiefly as an exploration of Prince Henry, now the profligate but soon to become the redeemer. Only Hal is always conscious of his obligations toward his future as king, and he is aware that his escapades are a temporary thing from which he may glean knowledge. The audience shares this awareness. In this connection Falstaff can be seen as a joker in Shakespeare's game of English history, serving in whichever capacity currently convenient for the playwright.

FALSTAFF AS A CONTRAST TO HOTSPUR

Because Hal and Hotspur will meet on the battlefield near the conclusion of *1 Henry IV*, Falstaff is a soldier. In this capacity he serves brilliantly to bring out several important aspects of the play. He draws our attention to the figurative tug-of-war going on over the prince, where he [Falstaff] and Hotspur, both endowed with larger-than-life dimensions, stand at either end of the rope. Their two sides resemble a medieval stage setting, Heaven at one side, Hell's Mouth on the other, and Prince Henry seemingly vacillating between the two. One important difference between Falstaff's and Hotspur's extremes is their patterns of movement. Hotspur knows little rest. He is always in motion, his mindset reflected in his speech patterns as well as his incessant walking about, his abrupt gestures, and his constant need to accomplish something. His personality is magnetic and infectious in its restlessness and in spite of all its blemishes. . . .

In direct opposition we see Falstaff. Where Hotspur is lithe, Falstaff is enormous, and Hal lets no opportunity for telling us so escape him. Neither does Falstaff. Already at our first glimpse of him, he establishes himself as stationary. Falstaff does not act, he is acted upon, and he lends himself willingly as a butt for the young Prince's jokes. Where Hotspur is a creature of light, Falstaff is one of "Diana's foresters, gentlem[a]n of the shade, [minion] of the moon." Falstaff will not stand if he can sit, nor sit if he can recline. His preoccupation is not with glory and honor, but rather with avoiding the consequences of their opposites. He tries his best not to pay his tavern bills, because probably Hal will pay them, and as for the more serious aspects of his life, "[S]hall there be gallows standing in England when thou art king? . . . Do not thou when thou art king hang a thief." When it comes to courage and honor, he shows little understanding of the mettle of a true soldier:

> But tell me, Hal, art not thou horribly afeard? Thou being heir apparent, could the world pick thee out three such enemies again, as that fiend Douglas, that spirit Percy, and that devil

Glendower? Art thou not horribly afraid? Doth not thy blood
thrill at it?

(*1 Henry IV,* II.iv.361–366)

Falstaff and Hotspur provide the two extremes, the two perfect backgrounds against which we see Hal's character develop, but the similarity between them is contrived. Shakespeare needs Falstaff's character to be a soldier in this play,
so he makes him one and draws as much from this con-
trivance as he can. Certainly the clown speaks in IV.ii, when
Falstaff's disreputable force is criticized. We never see these
soldiers, who look as if Falstaff "had unloaded all the gibbets
and pressed the dead bodies."[1] Their soldiering is a means to
Falstaff's usual end, creature comforts, and after Falstaff has
confided in the audience how he has made money on the
King's press, we cannot believe that any real men will become cannon fodder. They are a joke of the clown's and cannot be taken seriously. Moreover this treatment of the soldiers serves to put the rebellion in perspective. . . .

The very versatility of Falstaff suggests the stage clown at
work, but there has to be more consistency to Falstaff's character than to that of the other stage clowns. . . . In *1 Henry IV*
he is thoroughly lovable. It is impossible to resist his exces-
sive good humor and his ability to turn every situation to his
own advantage in the audience's eyes. . . .

FALSTAFF AND THE GAD'S HILL INCIDENT

The confrontation between Hal and Falstaff after the unfor-
tunate affair at Gad's Hill is a justly celebrated scene; it is exquisitely comic and opens possibilities for unending varieties of stage business and delightful twists. Falstaff knows
that he is about to be made the butt of yet another of Hal's
jokes, and he comes on stage prepared. His opening comments are those of the victim who has been most horribly
abused. He speaks to the audience over the heads of whoever is on stage with him, yet well aware that he is heard if
not completely understood by the other characters:

A plague of all cowards, I say, and a vengeance too, marry
and amen! Give me a cup of sack, boy. Ere I lead this life long,
I'll sew nether-stocks,[2] and mend them and foot them too. A
plague of all cowards! Give me a cup of sack, rogue; is there

---

1. The bodies of executed felons were often suspended in cages near the scene of the
crime until they rotted.   2. *nether-stocks* stockings at this time were cut out of material and sewed, not knitted

no virtue extant? . . . You rogue, here's lime³ in this sack too: there is nothing but roguery to be found in villainous man, yet a coward is worse than a cup of sack with lime in it. A villainous coward! . . . there lives not three good men unhanged in England, and one of them is fat, and grows old, God help the while.⁴ A bad world I say.

(1Henry IV, II.iv.111–129)

Falstaff ignores everybody but the serving-boy and speaks directly to the audience. We have long been party to the plans laid by Poins and the Prince, and we have also seen Falstaff's ignominious departure from the scene of the robbery. Furthermore, Hal and Poins have fired our curiosity as to how Falstaff will react, and now, when Falstaff reenters, we are itching to see how he will extricate himself from this predicament in one large piece. His first line of counterattack is a beautiful piece of strategy. When Hal finally speaks directly to him, he whirls on him and charges:

> *Prince.* How now, wool-sack, what mutter you?
> *Falstaff.* A king's son! If I do not beat thee out of thy kingdom with a dagger of lath,⁵ and drive all thy subjects afore thee like a flock of wild geese, I'll never wear hair on my face more. You, Prince of Wales!
> *Prince.* Why, you whoreson round man, what's the matter?
> *Falstaff.* Are you not a coward? Answer me to that—and Poins there?
>
> *(1 Henry IV,* II.iv.132–140)

Before there has been any opening for the opponents, Falstaff, in wounded majesty, has established himself as the deserted hero. When the Prince goads him about the booty, Falstaff embarks on his heroic tale of Gad's Hill. . . .

The speed of performance will leave the audience breathless and probably unable to remember the details, but it remains clear that Falstaff's professed prowess grows ever larger, and that he seems to have enmeshed himself in the Prince's net so tightly that he cannot well escape with dignity. The comedy is all the richer for both the conspirators and the audience because we have just witnessed the proceedings with our own eyes. Then suddenly Falstaff changes tack and serves up "three misbegotten knaves in Kendal green," who attacked him from the back in darkness so dense "thou couldst not see thy hand." This is too much for Hal, who stops feeding him lines and turns for an attack of

---

3. *lime* used to adulterate wine by giving it better color and taste   4. *God help the while* God help these times   5. *dagger of lath* wooden dagger

his own: "Why, how couldst thou know these men in Kendal green when it was so dark thou couldst not see thy hand?" Falstaff refuses to rise to the bait:

> *Prince.* Come, tell us your reason. What sayest thou to this?
> *Poins.* Come, your reason, Jack, your reason.
> *Falstaff.* What, upon compulsion? 'Zounds, and I were at the strappado, or all the racks[6] in the world, I would not tell you on compulsion.
>
> (*1 Henry IV*, II.iv.228–233)

Hal finally gives a short, to-the-point account of the proceedings and accuses Falstaff, but contrary to all expectations Falstaff worms his way out from under. . . .

Busy as he is with his verbal fray, he is always in contact with the audience and never forgets to throw us a remark or wink, or to include us with the other guests in the tavern as he addresses Hal and Poins. He never admits to being bested, but succeeds in emerging as Hercules and the lion both, and when Hal attempts to goad him again, he only offers, "Ah, no more of that, Hal, if thou lovest me," thus both closing the argument and brushing the whole thing aside as he makes ready for new mirth. . . .

THE "KING-PRINCE PLAY" AT THE BOAR'S HEAD

In II.iv.322, when Falstaff reenters after having seen the King's messenger, he is suddenly very knowledgeable about politics and the characters of the leaders of the rebellion. Shakespeare uses this short political discussion to remind us of Hotspur, and have us compare them both with Hal, but soon Falstaff turns the potential dangers to theatricality. He stage-manages the "play extempore" promised in line 276. Hal has to "practise an answer" before he is actually rebuked by the King, his father, and Falstaff as King Henry quickly provides everything necessary:

> This chair shall be my state,[7] this dagger my sceptre, and this cushion my crown. . . . Give me a cup of sack to make my eyes look red, that it may be thought I have wept, for I must speak in passion, and I will do it in King Cambyses' vein.[8] . . . [*to the Hostess, who has not been given a part before*] Weep not, sweet Queen, for trickling tears are vain.
>
> (*1 Henry IV*, II.iv.373–386 [my stage directions])

. . . He makes use of his new exalted position to put in many

---

6. *strappado . . . racks* forms of torture   7. *state* throne   8. *King Cambyses* main character in an earlier, ridiculous play

good words for himself. He is

> a virtuous man ... [a] good portly man, i'faith, and a corpulent; of a cheerful look, a pleasing eye, and a most noble carriage. ...

This self-glorification of Falstaff's becomes too much for Hal, who demands that they exchange parts. Falstaff takes it all in his stride, and asks both the on-stage audience and us in the house to be the judge of who makes the better king as well as the better prince. Hal wants the king's part to get back at Falstaff, but he is immediately bested. After he has given a lengthy catalogue of Falstaff's imperfections and abominations, but without mentioning his name, Falstaff delivers the answer that will enable him to continue his self-eulogy:

> I would your Grace would take me with you: whom means your Grace?
> *Prince.* That villainous abominable misleader of youth, Falstaff, that old white-bearded Satan.
> *Falstaff.* My lord, the man I know.
> <div align="right">(<i>1 Henry IV</i>, II.iv.454–458)</div>

He then proceeds to number all the negative qualities Falstaff has succeeded in making endearing to us, because we know that he is no realistic person, he is our stage clown. We are so taken with this Falstaff, who is given adjectives such as "sweet," "kind," "true," and "valiant," that the threat of banishment with which Hal closes the play extempore may easily escape us. Falstaff the clown certainly chooses to ignore it, though the remark is addressed to him. With this line, Hal steps out of both his roles, and he addresses the audience self-consciously in anticipation of the future. ...

The mood of this tavern scene is as light and happy as anyone could desire, and it stands forth brilliantly against the serious background of the King's worries over the succession and the looming rebellion and civil war. Nothing serious is allowed a firm foothold, and should anything threaten this almost magical sphere, it is soon averted or turned to mirth. This is all Falstaff's doing. His fertile brain and nimble tongue, his ability to sustain long monologues, and his apparent control over his entire environment make comedy sparkle and shine. Falstaff is firmly established with the spectators as a clown extraordinary, whose every appearance later will be greeted with delight and high expectations. The Boar's Head scene stands forth so sharply because of Falstaff's ability to distance himself and this night

of merrymaking from reality, and to create theatre-within-
theatre twice over. For what is the recital of great deeds at
Gad's Hill but a long-sustained comic show carried by one
man? The clown provides us with comic fiction within the
fictitious history play. . . .

FALSTAFF PREPARES FOR BATTLE

Falstaff's most interesting clown performance in the history
plays can be found in the fifth act of *1 Henry IV.* Here he is all
clown, and uses all the tricks of his trade. His first appearance
is in the first scene, in preparation for the battle of Shrewsbury. We find him in the company of his betters and he is
mostly silent, but his one remark indicates that the Prince has
a difficult time trying to keep him quietly in his place:

> *Worcester.*   For I protest
> I have not sought the day of this dislike.
> *King.* You have not sought it? How comes it, then?
> *Falstaff.* Rebellion lay in his way, and he found it.
> *Prince.* Peace, chewet,[9] peace!
>
> (*1 Henry IV,* V.i.25–29)

Falstaff's remark, thrown to the audience and overheard by
the Prince, gives us a humorous angle on the making of
rebels. But Hal, firmly within the frame of the fiction, sees the
possibility for offense to Worcester and silences Falstaff. . . .

The more valiant and honorable the proceedings, the
more signals Falstaff will send to the audience about his
own distrust in all this lofty stuff. After the formal talks end
and Hal refuses to "bestride [him]" should he stumble during the coming battle, a fear emerges with which we can
sympathize: "I would t'were bedtime, Hal, and all well."
When Hal brushes him off and leaves him alone with us,
Falstaff first works on his courage, then gives it up and delivers his honest opinion about honor:

> Well, 'tis no matter, honour pricks me on.[10] Yea, but how if
> honour prick me off[11] when I come on, how then? Can honour
> set a leg? No. Or an arm? No. Or take away the grief of a wound?
> No. Honour hath no skill in surgery then? No. What is honour?
> A word. What is in that word Honour? What is honour? Air. A
> trim reckoning! Who hath it? He that died a-Wednesday. Doth
> he feel it? No. Doth he hear it? No. 'Tis insensible, then? Yea, to
> the dead. But will it not live with the living? No. Why? Detrac-
> tion will not suffer it. Therefore I'll none of it. Honour is a mere

9. *chewet* a jackdaw, a Eurasian crow   10. *honour pricks me on* honor spurs me forward to heroism   11. *prick me off* mark me down on the casualty list

scutcheon—and so ends my catechism.

(1 Henry IV, V.i.129–141)

Like Feste and Launcelot Gobbo[12] in their discussions with themselves, Falstaff has to make himself into two persons for this speech. On the one hand he presents a youthful, innocent aspect, on the other an old man's disillusioned one, but the issue is never truly in doubt. Worldly experience wins the day; death is grim, and if death is the price, Falstaff wants nothing to do with honor....

FALSTAFF AND THE HOTSPUR-HAL DUEL

The audience is now more than familiar with Falstaff's attitude towards battle, honor, and glory. With this firmly fixed in our minds nothing could be more beautifully timed than his entry in V.iv in the midst of the duel between the two most honorable and glory-seeking characters, Hotspur and Hal: "Well said, Hal! To it, Hal! Nay, you shall find no boy's play here, I can tell you." James L. Calderwood says of this entry:

> For a disconcerting moment or two we may realize that "boy's play" is precisely what we shall find, *are* finding, here—mock combat, bated swords, the carefully rehearsed thrust and riposte, with Hotspur maneuvering surreptitiously to let Hal stab him in the vest pocket where a small bladder of pig's blood is concealed to make the groundlings grunt and the ladies squeal. Boy's play is as prominent here as it is a bit later when Douglas rushes on stage to pursue that great bladder of blood and sherris, the squealing Falstaff, who saws the air with his sword while hunting a comfortable place to collapse in mortal agony.

Indeed, this is a spot where theatre and history meet and clash, and the clash will become louder still. Hal and Hotspur have uplifted our patriotic souls more than once, and never higher than in their precombat courtesies towards each other. But how can even such glory stand against a Falstaff on the sidelines, shouting encouragements and reminding the audience that this is after all only historical fiction. We see the well-known clown pattern in full flower here. Part of the clown's function is taking care that the audience does not become too deeply involved emotionally, and so he provides us with the possibility of a cooler and more analytical outside view....

---

12. Feste is the fool in Shakespeare's *Twelfth Night*, Gobbo the clown in *The Merchant of Venice*.

The mock-combat between Falstaff and Douglas runs parallel with the deadly serious one between Hal and Hotspur. Falstaff and Hotspur fall at about the same moment during the battle and on the same stage, but worlds apart. Hotspur dies firmly fixed within the fiction, maintaining his character to the very last. . . .

Falstaff can easily make it clear to us that he is keeping an eye on the goings on from his state of feigned death, partly to make sure that Hotspur is safely dead, and partly in order that the audience shall not become too absorbed in the proceedings. Once he gets back on his feet, he first lectures the audience on "counterfeiting," but then remembers that Hotspur is lying close by, and his fear returns:

> 'Zounds, I am afraid of this gunpowder Percy, though he be dead; how if he should counterfeit too and rise? By my faith, I am afraid he would prove the better counterfeit; therefore I'll make him sure, yea, and I'll swear I killed him. Why may not he rise as well as I? Nothing confutes me but eyes, and nobody sees me: therefore sirrah, with a new wound in your thigh, come you along with me.
>
> (*1 Henry IV*, V.iv.120–128)

His plan clearly is formed as he speaks. First he winces away from Hotspur in fear, but gradually Hotspur becomes less of the hero and more a mere corpse to Falstaff. He approaches him slowly, and finally addresses him familiarly and stabs him in the thigh. So much for glory and honor. But the truly interesting clown observations are on "counterfeiting." Falstaff reminds us that after this scene is over, the actor playing Hotspur will indeed rise just as Falstaff did, but out of our sight, for Hotspur belongs in the fiction. This whole speech is addressed to the audience, for there is nobody else to hear; still, the audience is also made a fiction of, for "nobody sees me." Falstaff juggles the world of the fiction and the world of the audience back and forth with great speed and dexterity and succeeds in making a mockery of everything heroic. The mere thought of what the explosive Hotspur would have said and done had he known of this is enough to set one laughing.

As Falstaff is getting a good grip on Hotspur's dead body, the two Princes enter, and our mirth rises as Hal says, "[T]hou art not what thou seem'st," and Falstaff replies, "No, that's certain." This is true on more levels than one. Falstaff is in reality an actor in a play, as he has just reminded us, but he also had been declared dead, which is obviously not the case, and now he claims to have killed Hotspur. Nothing is what it seems. . . .

Falstaff is one of Shakespeare's most brilliant clown figures. He has the space and the scope to shine forth in all manner of functions and to create laughter from the most incredible situations. Still he serves as an aspect of Hal's character formation, and he is never allowed to transcend that role. He is never given the close intimacy of Poins, he remains temptation refused, and he never succeeds in undermining Hal's credibility as the rightful heir. If anything, he lends to the future King Henry a depth of humanity on which he depends in *Henry V.* Moreover, Falstaff acts as a counterweight to Hotspur, and Shakespeare often puts them in parallel situations. In each of these, Falstaff's mockery provides the audience with a more detached view of the proceedings, a distance of which we are much in need. Hotspur without Falstaff would be a compelling character and much too serious competition for the Prince. So again we see the stage clown as our teacher and guide as well as the provider of mirth and enjoyment. If any one character opens our eyes and makes us see clearer, he is Falstaff.

Contrasts in *1 Henry IV*

F.J.G. Meehan

F.J.G. Meehan explains that Shakespeare added to and revised his historical sources to create contrasts in *1 Henry IV*. In particular, Meehan analyzes character contrasts within Prince Hal (Harry of Monmouth) and between Prince Hal and Hotspur (Harry Percy) as well as contrasts in settings and scenes. In his doctoral dissertation submitted to the faculty of the Catholic University of America, F.J.G. Meehan investigated the extent to which Shakespeare shaped his historical materials to emphasize dramatic contrasts.

The two plays of *King Henry IV* and the play of *King Henry V* might be appropriately styled the Prince Hal[1] Trilogy, for Harry of Monmouth, Prince of Wales and afterward King of England, is their undisputed hero. The story they tell—a story made up of many strands and sometimes, as in the second drama of the trilogy, told haltingly enough—is the story of Prince Henry's life and fame and fortunes, of his relatives and companions and servants and enemies and friends. Prince Hal does not dominate the plays as compellingly and insistently as Gloucester dominates *King Richard III,* nor does he achieve and maintain his place as protagonist invested with the constantly growing pathos which appears in the figure of King Richard II; in the two plays of *King Henry IV* he shares his prominence with Hotspur[2] and Falstaff, but the dramas are so contrived that both Hotspur and Falstaff are closely bound up with the interests of the leading figure.

These three plays are further remarkable for embodying the only notable instances in the English historical dramas where Shakespeare from time to time bids the deep browed muse of history wait in the wings while he summons the

1. This prince, son of King Henry IV, is called by various names: Prince Hal, Harry, Prince Henry, and eventually King Henry V. 2. also called Harry Percy

Reprinted from "Contrast in Shakespeare's Historical Plays," by F.J.G. Meehan (Ph.D. diss., Catholic University of America, 1915).

115

muse of comedy to disport herself on the stage. The alternation of scenes grave and gay, which so deeply offended Voltaire and other continental critics, seems to be one of the heritages bequeathed to the English drama from the religious plays of the Middle Ages.... In those plays Shakespeare took a perceptible stride in his development as a dramatist; while continuing to follow his sources with a fair measure of closeness in the strictly historical scenes, he gave himself more latitude in the introduction and elaboration of humorous episodes.

For his historical scenes in *1 Henry IV* Shakespeare continued to draw freely upon Holinshed and derived a few unimportant details from the chronicle of Stowe;[3] for his comic scenes he is himself almost entirely responsible. True, he undoubtedly found some material for his Eastcheap and Gadshill episodes[4] in an old play entitled *The Famous Victories of Henry the Fifth*, which was acted as early as 1588 and which found its way into print in 1594....

The First Part of *King Henry IV* gives us a wealth of material for a discussion of Shakespeare's manipulation of his scenes and characters in the light of the theory of contrast—the theory, by the way, that comes nearest to explaining the dramatic value of alternating tragedy and comedy in the one play. The theory of contrast, applied to *1 Henry IV*, furnishes adequate reasons for Shakespeare's selections and rejections from Holinshed and for his very considerable expansion and remolding of the suggestions he adopted from *The Famous Victories*.

THE CHARACTER OF PRINCE HAL

In the person of the young Prince of Wales Shakespeare was supplied, ready-to-hand, with a character who involved contrasts within himself. It is pretty generally agreed upon by scholars that the stories of the Prince's youthful follies—stories that held their ground largely because of their inherent dramatic quality—had but a slender basis in actuality; but this Shakespeare was obviously not in a position to know. The chroniclers stressed young Henry's wild oats era and so did the old play, and Shakespeare eagerly accepted a version that involved the striking contrast of a man who, leading a

---

3. Both Holinshed and Stowe wrote histories of England called *Chronicles*.   4. the episodes involving Falstaff

wild and tumultuous life as the son of the King, forthwith becomes a model man and a brilliant ruler when he ascends the throne.

Shakespeare accepted this version, but he did so with a difference. Throughout the play he takes pains to impress us with the belief that Henry is in the slums but not of them, that he associates with the scum and riffraff of London society and yet keeps himself unspotted of the mad world in which he takes his pleasure. Into the mouth of the Prince he puts a clear and explicit declaration of motives:

> I know you all, and will a while uphold⁵
> The unyoked humour⁶ of your idleness:
> Yet herein will I imitate the sun,
> Who doth permit the base contagious⁷ clouds
> To smother up his beauty from the world,
> That when he pleases again to be himself,
> Being wanted, he may be more wonder'd at,
> By breaking through the foul and ugly mists
> Of vapors that did seem to strangle him.
>
> .   .   .   .   .   .
>
> My reformation, glittering o'er my fault,
> Shall show more goodly and attract more eyes
> Than that which hath no foil to set it off.
> I'll so offend, to make offence a skill;
> Redeeming time⁸ when men think least I will.
>
> (I.ii.218–40)

A conventional criticism of these lines is that in them Prince Hal shows himself to be a good deal of a prig and a hypocrite, that he has not the mettle to face his faults like a man but gives himself specious reasons for doing the things he should not do. That criticism rests upon a misconception of the function of the soliloquy in which the lines appear. We find two distinct classes of soliloquies in Shakespeare— those which reveal the character and motives of the person thus thinking aloud and those which really constitute a direct statement of things to the audience. Now, in the soliloquy just quoted, Prince Hal seems to be revealing his own character and motives, he seems to be thinking aloud; but the soliloquy is in fact one of the other type, and the Prince is forced by his creator to engage in the ungrateful task of acting as his own chorus. Shakespeare, rather than the Prince, speaks to the audience; and he tells them, plainly

---

5. *uphold* tolerate   6. *unyoked humour* unrestrained behavior   7. *contagious* poisonous   8. *Redeeming time* making up for the time I have lost

enough to expect the unexpected, to be on the lookout for contrasts in the career of this scion of royalty. The device is crude and inartistic and as little dramatic here as it is when employed in the soliloquies of Faulconbridge in *King John;* but it does serve to call attention to the contrasts which, inhering in the life of the future King Henry V, make him a dramatic figure.

Note, too, that Shakespeare takes pains, in that soliloquy and elsewhere, to tone down the contrasts in Prince Hal's life; he is extremely careful to make of him an experimenter with vice, a taster rather than a thirster for the cup of iniquity. Had he, following his sources blindly, given us a Prince Hal who is a thoroughly bad lot, who is a brawler, a drunkard, a lecher, and a thief, and suddenly changed such a one into an ideal king, there would assuredly be contrast, but contrast that overleaps the bounds of probability. Theatrical often, but dramatic never, is the sudden conversion of villains. Some such contrast in the raw Shakespeare might have accepted in his apprentice days, the days that brought forth Talbot and la Pucelle; but now he was surer of himself and had learned the value of artistic repression. The numerous contrasts in *1 Henry IV* are not the blinding and unconvincing contrasts of black and white; the master has by this time learned somewhat the significance of shades and tones.

SHAKESPEARE REVISES PRINCE HAL'S VISIT TO HIS FATHER, HENRY IV

This is brought home to us by reflection on an omission that Shakespeare made when writing the second scene of Act III, an omission trivial enough in itself but suggestive as bearing on the development of the dramatist and on his manipulation of his sources. According to Holinshed, when the Prince went to the court, "apparelled in a gown of blue satin, full of small eyelet holes, at every hole the needle hanging by a silk thread, with which it was sewed," he was accompanied "with such a number of noblemen and other his friends that wished him well, as the like train had seldom been seen repairing to the court at any one time in those days." Going in alone to his father, "then grievously diseased," he knelt down and pleaded his affection and loyalty. He concluded by drawing his dagger after the fashion of Cassius in the tent at Sardis—extending it to the King and exclaiming: "I beseech you, most redoubled lord and dear father, for the honour of

God, to ease your heart of all such suspicion as you have of me, to despatch me here before your knees, with this same dagger." Verily, here was something to feast the eyes and split the ears of the groundlings; but Shakespeare left it out. He saw in it a contrast that would be dramatic in *Julius Caesar* but theatrical here. Instead, he constructed a scene stately in tempo and devoid of movement and yet which is absorbingly dramatic—the Bolingbroke, now King, who drove Richard from the throne, makes his peace with the son who has caused him grief. Beautifully does the King point out the contrast between his own youth and that of his wayward son:

> Had I so lavish of my presence been,
> So common hackney'd[9] in the eyes of men,
> So stale and cheap to vulgar company,
> Opinion, that did help me to the crown,
> Had still kept loyal to possession,[10]
> And left me in reputeless banishment,
> A fellow of no mark nor likelihood.
>
> .   .   .   .
>
> Thus did I keep my person fresh and new;
> My presence, like a robe pontifical,[11]
> Ne'er seen but wonder'd at: and so my state,
> Seldom but gumptious, showed like a feast,
> And won by rareness such solemnity.

(III.ii.39–59)

THE CHARACTER OF HOTSPUR

The dominant contrast in *1 Henry IV* is that between Prince Hal and Hotspur, a contrast which affords an excellent illustration of Shakespeare's selection from the material at his disposal and of his process of piecing out that material the better to subserve his ends. The Hotspur of history was a gallant soldier, and that is substantially all that is known of his personal traits. He was called Hotspur, according to one account, "from his much pricking"; according to another, "because, in the silence of the night, and while others reposed in sleep, he would labor indefatigably against his enemy, as if heating his spurs." But, historically, "the surname of Hotspur had no reference to his disposition of temper," which was a brilliant invention of the dramatist.

Admirable is the manner in which Shakespeare brings

---

9. *common hackney'd* at every man's call   10. *possession* possessor; i.e. Richard II
11. *robe pontifical* a bishop's robe

out the contrasting characters of the two Harrys. Though
they do not meet face to face until the decisive day at
Shrewsbury, all through the play the audience is forced to
keep them in mind and to institute a detailed comparison.
The difference between them is much in the King' thoughts,
and elements in the comparison are being furnished by re-
marks put into the mouths of the other characters; the two
Harrys, indeed, speak of each other, and in eminently characteristic style. As the "madcap Prince of Wales" is brought
into relief by contrasts with his father, his brother, and his
companions of the tavern, so "the Hotspur of the north; he
that kills me some six or seven doxen of Scots at a breakfast,
washes his hands, and says to his wife 'Fie upon this quiet
life! I want work,'" is made distinct and clear cut by a series
of contrasts with his slow going father, his foxy uncle, the
perfumed lordling, the wearisome Glendower, the winsome
Lady Percy. No historical warrant exists for Shakespeare's
presentation of Glendower as a bore against whom the practical, impatient Hotspur protests:

> O he is as tedious
> As a tired horse, a railing wife;
> Worse than a smoky house: I had rather live
> With cheese and garlick in a windmill, far,
> Than feed on cates[12] and have him talk to me
> In any summer house in Christendom.
>
> (III.i.159–164)

And the contrast between Hotspur and his wife—a contrast
which so finely sets in relief the abruptness and stubborn-
ness of the man—is likewise Shakespeare's invention; history records nothing more than the bare fact of Lady Percy's
existence.

With consummate art Shakespeare brings the contrasts of
the two Harrys to a splendid culmination on the field of
Shrewsbury. For the first time the rivals meet face to face. Ig-
noring the fact that the Hotspur of history was at the very
least as old as Prince Hal's father, Shakespeare heightens
and points the contrast by making them of the one age. Brief
and brilliant is their conversation; they fight, and Harry
Percy falls. "Adieu," cries the chivalrous victor, never more a
prince than now, "and take thy praise with thee to heaven!"
Here once more Shakespeare deviated from his sources;
Hotspur fell by an unknown hand.

12. *cates* delicacies

RICH CONTRASTING SCENES

If *1 Henry IV* is rich in contrasts of character, it is not less so in contrasts of scene. The tavern scenes, wherein the Prince appears often and Hotspur never, are set off against the home scenes, wherein Percy dominates and the Prince never intrudes. A further contrast exists between the court scenes and the battle scenes, in the former of which the two Harrys are flitting visitants, in the latter meeting for the only time in life. This is something more than the mere alternation of scenes grave and gay; it is the contrast, exquisitely shaded and blended, of four varying environments, each a background shaped and adapted for throwing into relief the people in the play. Two scenes in *1 Henry IV,* in both of which Shakespeare transcended his sources, merit special attention. One of them, the fourth scene in the fifth act, is as fine a presentation of the ironic contrasts of life as Shakespeare ever conceived. The two Harrys have fought, and Percy lies dead, "food for worms." Nearby lies Sir John Falstaff, feigning death. The hero of the north and the braggart of Eastcheap—he who had thought [in Hotspur's words]

> it were an easy leap,
> To pluck bright honour from the pale-faced moon,

and he who had declared that same honor to be "a mere scutcheon"—lie side by side; and the rigid body of the fiery Hotspur is presently borne off on the back of the chuckling knight. The spectacle recalls the words but a moment before uttered by the Prince:

> *Ill-weaved ambition,* how much art thou shrunk!
> When that this body did contain a spirit,
> A kingdom for it was too small a bound.[13]

(V.iv.88–90)

The other scene (II. iv.) has been declared, and apparently with justice, the most comical stage picture in Shakespeare. Through it contrasts, singly and in battalions, play back and forth; and while Mistress Quickly screams her admiration and Bardolph's nose shines beaconlike through the foetid air, Sir John Falstaff explains how it is that he was a coward on compulsion. And then, the same Sir John, the uncrowned king of Eastcheap, assumes for the nonce the trappings of mock royalty: "This chair shall be my state, this dagger my

---

13. *bound* boundary

sceptre, and this cushion my crown"; and forthwith he plays the Prince's father "in King Cambyses' vein." Nor is that all. Conditions are speedily reversed; the madcap Prince impersonates the King, Falstaff plays the Prince; and in that rôle saves the scene from anticlimax and carries it to a glorious fulness by his mock heroic plea—for himself: "Banish plump Jack, and banish all the world."

The Decline of the King in *2 Henry IV*

M.M. Reese

M.M. Reese traces the downfall of Henry IV, arguing
that Henry fails essentially because he judges by
appearances. Reese shows that the king's faulty
judgment causes him to misunderstand Prince Hal
and the rebels, who are as blind and weak as the
king. Henry dies without knowing that Hal will have
a better reign. M.M. Reese was a teacher, writer,
lecturer, and journalist. He is the author of *The
Tudors and the Stuarts* and *Shakespeare: His World
and His Work.*

> So shaken as we are, so wan with care,
> Find we a time for frighted peace to pant,
> And breathe short-winded accents of new broils
> To be commenc'd in stronds[1] afar remote....
> *—1 Hen. IV*, I i I.

The limp, exhausted rhythms of the opening speech announce the nature of Bolingbroke's England. Without any
direct allusion Shakespeare looks swiftly back to the events
of *Richard II* and sums up their meaning as he shows us this
tired and impotent king whom we last met in the confident
beginnings of his reign. This is the man who took a crown
because he would wear it better than the king he had deposed; and the quality of his act is to be judged by his decline
from efficiency and decisiveness to the haggard uncertainty
in which we find him now....

Here he is in angry conflict with the Percies, his allies in
the events that brought him to the throne. As Richard pre-
dicted, their common complicity in these events has now
locked them in a struggle that will be fatal to the country and
fatal to themselves. The Percies cannot forgive Henry for

1. *stronds* shores

From *The Cease of Majesty: A Study of Shakespeare's History Plays,* by M.M. Reese
(London: Edward Arnold, 1961). Reprinted with permission of the Estate of M.M.
Reese.

taking the richest prize: if he were to give them half the kingdom, Richard had said, they would think it too little, having helped him to win it all. The present relationship between them is therefore grounded in mutal fear: the Percies' fear that Henry, knowing them for what they are, will not rest until he has robbed them of their power to strike in the same way again; and Henry's corresponding fear that men who have been rebels once are likely to be rebels for evermore. It is a contest in which there can be no winners. Both sides are the helpless victims of their own past. . . .

HENRY BECOMES FATALISTIC

In Part Two Henry seems to lose all ambition to control events. Yielding to the pervasive decay and infirmity of the times, he sinks into a fatalism in which he wonders how things could have been persuaded to happen differently. In a scene which parallels Richard's spiritless collapse when both Carlisle and Aumerle tried to stir him to his duty (*Rich. II* III ii), Henry rejects Warwick's optimistic counsel that the 'rank diseases' of the kingdom may still be healed by determined physic. If we could read the book of fate, we should only learn that human effort is inevitably condemned to fail, and he will not be persuaded by Warwick's argument that the past does not irrevocably engage the future. Wisely read, Warwick says, it may be a guide to decisive action:

> There is a history in all men's lives,
> Figuring the nature of the times deceas'd;
> The which observ'd, a man may prophesy,
> With a near aim, of the main chance of things
> As yet not come to life.
>
> (*II Hen IV* III i 80)

But Henry only answers him with apathetic resignation ('Are these things then necessities? Then let us meet them like necessities.') and a further reference to his crusade, the illusory ideal in which he tries to find some emotional compensation for his failure. The open misconduct of the heir [Prince Hal] is additional punishment for his fault, and he expects nothing but ruin for the country when he is dead.

> The blood weeps from my heart when I do shape
> In forms imaginary the unguided days
> And rotten times that you shall look upon
> When I am sleeping with my ancestors.
> For when his headstrong riot hath no curb,
> When rage and hot blood are his counsellors. . . .
>
> (*II Hen IV* IV iv 58)

... The rebels are in even worse case than the King, being subject to the blindness and paralysis of will that inevitably accompanied rebellious acts. They too carry the crushing burden of past wrongdoing, and throughout the two parts of the play they drift helplessly towards a defeat which they have expected for so long that it no longer has any meaning for them. ...

Worcester admits, in fact, that rebellion is conceived in passion and cannot stand up to rational examination: its adherents, inevitably, are deluded men. Of this point he is soon to give a personal demonstration, for it is he who suppresses Henry's offer of peace, thinking in his passionate blindness that it cannot be sincere. His words show too how rebellion is vulnerable to the sort of rumour, or false report, that is described in the Induction to Part Two. Sedition breeds 'surmises, jealousies, conjectures', and is itself destroyed by its own offspring. The action then begins with a post-mortem on the defeat of Shrewsbury. ... The rebels greet the Archbishop of York as a powerful convert to their cause, assuring each other that his presence will overcome all religious objections to the enterprise, but they soon discover that they have only recruited another fatalist. Although engaged to 'consecrate commotion's bitter edge', he speaks of the rising in tones of extreme distaste and disillusion. He regards the whole thing as the manifestation of a diseased surfeiting— the people who were once tired of Richard are tired now of Bolingbroke.

> The commonwealth is sick of their own choice;
> Their over-greedy love hath surfeited.[2]
> A habitation giddy and unsure
> Hath he that buildeth on the vulgar heart.[3] ...
>   What trust is in these times?
>   (*II Hen IV* I iii 87)

Later in the play, when Westmoreland has denounced rebellion and asked how a respected prelate, 'whose beard the silver hand of peace hath touch'd', comes to be mixed up in it, the Archbishop once again speaks of it as a universal disease.

>   We are all diseas'd;
> And, with our surfeiting and wanton[4] hours
> Have brought ourselves into a burning fever,
> And we must bleed for it.
>   (*II Hen IV* IV i 54)

---

2. *surfeited* overeaten, gone to excess   3. *vulgar heart* the love of the people   4. *surfeiting and wanton* gluttonous and frivolous

. . . The Archbishop regards the King and his party, equally with the rebels, as the powerless victims of circumstance. The men who are now posing as the defenders of society were rebels once themselves, and their present show of righteousness cannot protect them from their past.

It is in this picture of impotent confusion that Shakespeare finally presents the nemesis of rebellion. Both sides, the adherents of the established order as well as its enemies, feel themselves to be the dumb actors of roles that necessity has prescribed. They are victims of a general malady; or, as they more often think of it, they are the sport of Time. Especially in Part Two, Time is the dominant symbol of the play, and all the characters confess their helplessness as Time's subjects. Life itself is just Time's fool, and Hotspur will accept death as release from its tyranny. In this common subjection to Mutability, rebels and royalists seem to lose all separate identity and become, as Mr. D.A. Traversi has said, 'complementary aspects of a dramatic unity conceived by the poet in terms of the rooted infirmity which threatens society with dissolution'. The final sickness of rebellion is a universal impotence in which it no longer matters who is a foe and who a friend. . . .

THE PUBLIC AND PRIVATE KING

As the author of a violent past, [Henry IV] was condemned to be the victim of a violent present, bound with the rebels in an endless chain of circumstance. He could not rule as the strong, pacific king that he had hoped to be, and his plan for a crusade, through which he might expiate his sin, would never be more than an ironically distant mirage. His daily problem was simply to find a means of keeping by force what force had won him.

Long before the end the proud and confident Bolingbroke has shrunk into a sleepless neurotic helplessly revolving the theme of 'if only we had known'. But this was a weakness that he revealed only to his family and the few counsellors he could trust. The public Henry is never unimpressive, and Shakespeare lets us feel that here is a shrewd, courageous man doing his best in conditions in which, through his own original fault, success was impossible. . . . His is a threadbare, makeshift majesty, and his idea of statesmanship aims no higher than the devious manipulation of opposing forces. He is a sort of poor man's Machiavelli,[5] using the gifts and dedicated purpose of political man simply to keep himself in power.

HENRY MISUNDERSTANDS PRINCE HAL

Nothing is more typical of his limited understanding than his failure to perceive his son's true nature. He does not understand Falstaff or Hotspur either, for he is a man who judges by appearances. This, as he now realises, had been his mistake before he took the throne, when he misjudged the Percies and perhaps misjudged Richard too. But he has not learned wisdom from his failure, and at their first meeting in the play he treats Hal to an extended lecture on the importance of wearing the right sort of public face. . . .

He goes on to tell the Prince how he won the throne, by an affectation of courtesy and humility that kept his person ever 'fresh and new'. . . . Henry is admitting his son into the tricky secret of how he formerly drew attention to himself by a policy of deliberate effacement. It has nothing to do with royalty as Hal is coming to understand it, and he makes no comment whatever upon these seamy disclosures. In fact his reply is a definite rebuke:

> I shall hereafter, my thrice gracious lord,
> *Be more myself.*

(I Hen IV III ii 92)

Shortly before he dies Henry begs Clarence to use his personal influence with Hal and to encourage those good qualities in him that may restrain his passions. But Henry is by this time too defenceless and disillusioned to have any sanguine hopes about the future, and he continues to torment himself by imagining 'the unguided days and rotten times' that will come after him. These anxieties seem to be confirmed when he finds the Prince prematurely wearing the crown, and he falls again into the prolonged and nagging self-pity that would have justified any of his sons in keeping out of his way.

> Pluck down my officers, break my decrees;
> For now a time is come to mock at form[6]
> Harry the Fifth is crown'd! Up, vanity!
> Down, royal state![7] all you sage counsellors, hence!
> And to the English court assemble now,
> From every region, apes of idleness!

(II Hen IV IV v 116)

5. Italian political philosopher and author of *The Prince*   6. *form* order   7. *state* the formal dignity of the state

He forgets, apparently, the continuous disorder that his own reign has been, and on and on he goes, declaring that Harry will pluck from curb'd licence the muzzle of restraint until, with appetite roaming unrebuked, the country will again be peopled by its old inhabitants, the wolves.

This is Henry in his accustomed vein, and the significant passage in the scene occurs when he has swiftly and without question accepted the Prince's explanation of his putting on the crown. Persuaded at last that Hal does not intend to waste the crown in dissipation, he gathers his strength to utter 'the very latest counsel that ever I shall breathe': the final witness of a king. . . .

> Therefore, my Harry,
> Be it thy course to busy giddy minds
> With foreign quarrels; that action, hence borne out,[8]
> May waste the memory of the former days.
>   (*II Hen IV* IV v 211)

The Prince is thus advised to seek an excuse for campaigns overseas, as a means of preventing civil war at home, but once again he avoids direct comment on these proposals. To Henry's final prayer that he may be permitted to keep this dubious crown in peace, he [Hal] simply answers,

> My gracious liege,
> You won it, wore it, kept it, gave it me;
> Then plain and right must my possession be:
> Which I with more than with a common pain[9]
> 'Gainst all the world will rightfully maintain.
>   (*II Hen IV* IV v 219)

These pantomime couplets announce the indefeasible rights of possession, a commonplace upon which even King John was able to insist. It is in the circumstances the only conceivable answer, a public and formal acceptance of responsibility. What is significant is that Hal refuses complicity in his father's idea of statecraft.

Hal is moving in the youthful gravity with which he lays the heavy burden on his head; and even if his previous uncertain relationship with his father makes him protest too much when he explains his action, he leaves no doubt of the spirit of dedication in which he admits the due of 'tears and heavy sorrows of the blood'. Joy and vainglorious pride are altogether absent as he receives the crown as an enemy whose cares have killed his father. He takes it as a trust too

---

8. *hence born out* i.e., in foreign lands   9. *pain* labor

sacred to be soiled by the politic advice to which he has just been compelled to listen, and his submission to the Lord Chief Justice, in which he formally recants the wildness of his youth, has deeper significance as a repudiation of his father's devious ways:

> There is my hand:
> You shall be as a father to my youth;
> My voice shall sound as you do prompt mine ear,
> And I will stoop and humble mine intents
> To your well-practis'd wise directions.
> And, princes all, believe me, I beseech you;
> My father is gone wild into his grave,
> For in his tomb lie my affections;
> And with his spirit sadly I survive,
> To mock the expectation of the world,
> To frustrate prophecies, and to raze out
> Rotten opinion, who hath writ me down
> After my seeming. The tide of blood in me
> Hath proudly flow'd in vanity till now:
> Now doth it turn and ebb back to the sea,
> Where it shall mingle with the state of floods
> And flow henceforth in formal majesty.
>
> (*II Hen IV* V ii 117)

Hal has accepted the principles of justice and the rule of law, and as the bearer of a title in which there was no personal dishonour he would be able to rise above the shifts of 'policy'. It is his final test and his greatest victory. Neither Falstaff's fleshly seductions nor Hotspur's envious emulation have attached him in quite the same way as the claims of kinship and office exerted by his father, and it would have been easy for an inexperienced youth to confuse craftiness with statesmanship and accept Henry's separation between the private and public faces of a ruler. Hal recognises this attitude to be false, but without absolutely denying Commodity's place in the conduct of society: there are times when the most honest of rulers has to dissemble and times when he must be more ruthless than a private citizen need ever be.

Hal will be a good king because events have schooled him in knowledge and responsibility.

Two Levels of Meaning in *2 Henry IV*

A.R. Humphreys

Beneath the action and dialogue of *2 Henry IV*, says A.R. Humphreys, Shakespeare has created a picture of English moral life during Henry IV's time. Humphreys bridges the literal level and the social portrayal by discussing topics not readily discernible in the characters' speeches and action but present nonetheless: the morality of effective rule, rumor and miscalculation, anarchy, age and disease, and city and rural life. A.R. Humphreys had a long teaching career at Leicester University. He was a research fellow at the Folger Shakespeare Library in Washington, D.C., the author of *Shakespeare's "Merchant of Venice,"* and an editor of *Henry V, Henry VIII, Much Ado About Nothing,* and *Julius Caesar.*

The New Variorum edition [of *2 Henry IV*] presents an interesting range of estimates of the plays, from H.N. Hudson's 'Everyone, upon reading these two dramas, must be sensible of a falling-off in the latter' to R.G. White's claim that 'it is unsurpassed in its combination of variety and perfection by any other production of his pen'. . . .

However that may be, Shakespeare shows every sign of strong interest, from the lines in which Rumour conjures up a nation in tumult, through the tragic urgency of Northumberland's and Morton's exchanges and the council of war, to the confrontation of the opponents. Henry appears late and infrequently, but there is a moving power in his utterance. Falstaff lacks Hal, but his exchanges with the Lord Chief Justice, Mistress Quickly, and Shallow are boldly impudent. . . . Part 2 is hardly less powerful as an act of the imagination, with a vitality and indeed violence in its comedy, a passion and thoughtfulness in its history, without which the canon

From *The Second Part of* King Henry IV, edited by A.R. Humphreys (London: Methuen, 1966). Reprinted by permission of the publisher.

of the plays would be much the poorer. It is unified by the powerful treatment of a nexus of themes. . . .

MORALITY AND EFFECTIVE RULE

In *2 Henry IV* the King certainly suffers from remorse; he yearns for an expiatory crusade, he admits 'indirect crook'd ways', and he prays God for forgiveness, as his son prays on the eve of Agincourt that God will not visit upon him 'the fault / My father made in compassing the crown'. Yet the sense behind the play, and in Henry's mind, is not one *primarily* of remorse afflicting him but of anxiety over political unrest. Henry's anguish has to do with his usurpation, but it centres mostly on Hal's wildness which threatens to lose the crown to rivals. Henry's worries are superimposed on a troubled conscience; yet one feels that if the worries would abate the conscience would settle itself too. The play is one of practical power, with Divine Right in a very minor place. . . .

Behind the plays there are the potent symbols of the Wheel of Fortune and Mutability,[1] factors of fatalism. But in the foreground there is practical and secular Necessity, calling forth the will. The plays are not primarily religious parables of God's wrath for sin, or mythopoems of Mutability; they deal with men who elect to do what they deem necessary actions. The King acts so, but so also do the rebels— 'Necessity' is their very natural plea. Henry is 'guilty' of not resisting the events which bring him to power; yet he is justified in that he was 'compell'd' to act so. . . . The mainspring is secular, practical, the ensuring of success; and guilt in a religious sense runs second to guilt against the codes of political order. And to this second guilt Henry can reply that he meant to bring political order, not to destroy it.

Yet to judge that the only criterion is success or failure, 'Is the King strong or weak?', is too narrow. Success or failure is of course important to monarchs. But behind the success or failure some moral significance should be felt. Behind Henry's success, blemished though it is, there must be a larger welfare than the dynastic, and this must indeed be more than the mere national magnification of his personal success. It must be the whole welfare of the state, the great living order which is expressed here by those who oppose the Archbishop of York and in *Henry V* in the Archbishop of

---

1. *Mutability* changeableness; inconstancy

Canterbury's honey-bees speech. Behind the rebels' failure there must likewise be some moral fitness; their lack of cohesion, their well-meant recklessness, would have augured ill for the nation had they won. . . .

Henry IV and *Henry V,* in [critic H.B.] Charlton's view, reveal 'a distinctly contemptuous view of statesmen and statecraft'. Is this true?

Surely it is not. . . . The theme is not the contemptibility of statesmen but Hal's emergence to good rule. Good rule is not the wielding of power but the fostering of the good life on a national scale. That is what a king is for. . . . The King here is less prominent than in Part I but he is anything but contemptible. The complexities of right and wrong in his usurpation continue in his exercise of power, and the responsibilities of rule, rendered harsh by his own acts, and his capacity for melancholy analysis, ally him with the flawed heroes of the tragedies. . . .

The royal representatives exemplify Justice, which the Elizabethans enshrined among the highest virtues. It could have its Aristotelian excess, mean, and defect.[2] John and Westmoreland represent its extreme, the justice which metes without mercy what each deserves; such justice is needed in statecraft but only in emergencies. . . . If rigour is one extreme, anarchy (the defect of justice) is the other, adumbrated in Falstaff's prospects, trumpeted in his cry 'the laws of England are at my commandment'. . . . If these, then, are divergent extremes from firm but merciful authority, the Lord Chief Justice embodies those qualities which Hal requires, good government in the microcosm of man and the macrocosm of the state. . . .

Statesmen and statecraft are not, then, held to be by nature contemptible. Daily exigencies may tarnish the kingly function, as the burden of rule oppresses kings themselves, but on the earthly plane good statecraft is the highest of human exercises, that 'hard condition / Twin-born with greatness / in which men show likest gods when they rule with honour to their place and with the love of their subjects. The moral centre of the sequence from *Richard II* to *Henry V* is the nature and the gravity of rule. Shakespeare has made his plays most thoughtful enactments of the art of the possible.

---

2. In his *Ethics,* Aristotle advocates the principle of the golden mean (moderation) as better than excess (too much) or defect (too little).

MISCALCULATION

One of the most evident themes is that of miscalculation. The play is introduced by Rumour, spirit of unrest and false knowledge. The chronicles say nothing about Northumberland's hearing deceptive reports from Shrewsbury, and Shakespeare's invention of Rumour is a pure imaginative device, to create the world of 'surmises, jealousies, conjectures'. On the serious level, most of the characters could cry out with the Archbishop, 'What trust is in these times?' or, with the King, 'how chance's mocks / And changes fill the cup of alteration / With divers liquors'. On the comic level, there is the vague belief that Falstaff performed valiantly at Shrewsbury; the Lord Chief Justice refers to it, warriors seek the hero out, Colevile surrenders without a blow (and is executed, a disturbing switch from histrionic farce to historic fact). Living on a false reputation, Falstaff himself hubristically miscalculates Hal. At the centre, of course, is Hal's intention to surprise everyone:

> So, when this loose behaviour I throw off,
> And pay the debt I never promised,
> By how much better shall my word I am
> By so much shall I falsify men's hopes.
>
> (*I Henry IV* I. ii. 232–5)

Optimistic and pessimistic, falsified hopes (i.e. expectations) spread throughout the play. Insofar as it concerns Hal himself, the dramatic expectancy lies in the anticipations of him so variously entertained by the King on the one hand, and Falstaff on the other. But there are other aspects of the same theme. The rebels' war-council is equally concerned with the unpredictable future; they are betrayed dangerously when Northumberland abandons them and disastrously when they miscalculate Prince John. To sum up, the rebels are tragically foiled of their expectations, Falstaff and Shallow comically foiled of theirs, and the King and Lord Chief Justice fortunately foiled of theirs. Only Hal, 'Machiavel of goodness', is not Time's or Fortune's fool.

ANARCHY

Other themes interplay in both serious and comic plots to give coherence. Anarchy threatens throughout. The rebels and Falstaff both prepare it; the King expects it on Hal's accession, and he anticipates disorder.... The Archbishop, though nobler in his impulses than Northumberland, pro-

FAL. My King! My Jove! I speak to thee, my heart!
K. HEN. V. I know thee not, old man. Fall to thy prayers.
How ill white hairs become a fool and jester!
I have long dreamed of such a kind of man,
So surfeit-swelled,[1] so old, and so profane,
But, being awaked, I do despise my dream.
Make less thy body hence, and more thy grace.
Leave gormandizing. Know the grave doth gape
For thee thrice wider than for other men.
Reply not to me with a fool-born jest.
Presume not that I am the thing I was,
For God doth know, so shall the world perceive,
That I have turned away my former self,
So will I those that kept me company.
When thou dost hear I am as I have been,
Approach me, and thou shalt be as thou wast,
The tutor and the feeder of my riots.
Till then, I banish thee, on pain of death,
As I have done the rest of my misleaders,
Not to come near our person by ten mile.
For competence of life[2] I will allow you,
That lack of means enforce you not to evil.
And as we hear you do reform yourselves,
We will, according to your strength and qualities,
Give you advancement. Be it your charge, my lord,
To see performed the tenor[3] of our word.
Set on.

1. *surfeit-swelled* swollen through overeating 2. *competence of life* means to live
3. *tenor* purpose

poses to throw England into the melting-pot of popular fickleness. For Falstaff, of course, the law of nature decrees that the old pike should snap up the young dace;[3] he devours the rustic recruits and Shallow alike without the slightest semblance of exertion, and he prepares short shrift for the Lord Chief Justice and the laws of the land. A common courting of chaos moves rebels and Falstaff alike.

3. *dace* a fish metaphor describing Falstaff's behavior, Falstaff being the pike, the recruits being the dace, or small fish

AGE AND DISEASE

Northumberland and the King, the main participants in Richard's overthrow, are physically afflicted as well as morally blemished; Shallow and Silence are captivatingly senile; and 'in Falstaff the comedy of ageing flesh is grotesque as well as amusing'. Not all the elders, certainly, are unsound; the Archbishop, though an unskilful leader, is a noble prelate, the 'opener and intelligencer' between God and man; and the Lord Chief Justice is worthy to be a king's guardian. Hal will surround himself with wise veterans, as *Henry V* shows him to have done—'The silver livery of advised age' was always a moving idea to Shakespeare. But the old blemished order must change; the new King must show himself part of the nation's healthy rather than its failing stock. Until he does so, however, age and disease affect the body politic; this theme is common to the King and Archbishop alike. As for Falstaff, he turns diseases to commodity, and he flirts with Doll through a desire which has long outlived performance. He is far from senile, but the 'vanity in years' feels shadows of mortality. And he and the tavern-life centring upon him are now, as they were not in Part I, too deeply blemished for a prince's health. He is master of his court, but of a court much grosser, less gay, and more salacious. The tavern-comedy is splendidly vivacious; the great Boar's-Head scene, the last gathering of the whole company at Eastcheap, is given with a creative enthusiasm which averts the censoriousness some critics have sought to pin upon Shakespeare. Still, wonderful though its reading of life, its themes of age and disease link with those of the serious plot in a symbolic rendering of the state of England.

THE PANORAMA OF ENGLISH LIFE

Of all the plays, this most richly draws the panorama of national life. The troubled kingdom is evoked in many a speech from Rumour's onwards, and the contrasting ideal community is expounded by Westmoreland, Prince John, the Lord Chief Justice, and the new King himself. There is varied and vigorous movement throughout the land. The military scenes show a nation swarming with the concerns of war; topographical and social references abound; messengers ride and armies march. Outside the history plot, Mistress Quickly seems the very embodiment of her Eastcheap neighbourhood, and Doll is as common as the St Albans road. Shallow, whose cousin is at Oxford, equally embodies Old England, recalling his days at Clement's Inn with little John Doit of Staffordshire and Will Squele, a Cotsole man, when he took on Samson Stockfish behind Gray's Inn while Jack Falstaff, page to the Duke of Norfolk, was breaking Scoggin's head at the court gate. Bullocks are sold at Stamford, sacks lost at Hinckley fair; William Visor of Woncot needs help against Clement Perkes o'the Hill. The Gloucestershire scenes have been called a glorious irrelevance. But are they? The hero of the history plays is the nation; the theme is the state of England. The idea that Eastcheap is an irrelevance has long been given up; so should any such idea about Gloucestershire, which is the rural counterpart of East-cheap, allied with the rest of the play by its themes of justice and war working down to the common folk, and by its rendering of common life proceeding in quotidian tragi-comedy behind the self-importance of the great. 'In *Henry IV*, which is so much more than a political play, the public situation is defined and judged in terms of a richly human context in which Falstaff's ragged regiment and the Cotswold conscripts are an indispensable part.' Eastcheap and Gloucestershire together present the heart-warming common stock of things. Mistress Quickly and Davy, as Dr Tillyard observes, are comforting assurances that 'civil war will yield, as the play's main theme, to England'. And if the whole panorama is spread out, from Pie Corner in Eastcheap to the Gloucestershire hade land to be sown with red wheat, from Poins's tennis-court to Northumberland's castle, if messengers devour the way, and Falstaff founders nine score and odd posts between the Boar's Head and Gaultree, the topography is a matter not merely of the passing moment but of a fully rendered local colour, of history seen in the events of men's lives.

TIME

Furthermore, the play embeds itself in a deep layer of time. Time has two main aspects—the present as it presses towards the future, the past as it revives in the present. In the former aspect, it presses towards finality, precipitating the rebels' plans and the King's counter-plans. Hal feels himself much to blame, 'so idly to profane the present time'. The urgent observation of time which weighs upon men in high places is a major part of the play's stress, and even the life of the tavern, though trying to ignore it, is more under its sway than in Part I. Scarcely any play has so definite a *terminus ad quem*,[4] for all parties 'the stream of time doth run' towards a conclusion. 'In the perfectness of time' Hal is to reign, and this event impends with fear in the mind of the court, glee in that of the tavern, and gravity in his own. Moreover, the present pressing towards the future is not only insistent, it is inexorable. It brings those revolutions of the times against which, for all his planning, man cannot secure himself. Even beyond 'the victorious acts of Henry the Fifth' there loom the further troubles foreseen by Northumberland and prophesied by Hastings. Above all, it brings age and death, and it is in deeply admitting this quality of time that the play takes on its sombre grandeur.

But the second aspect of time, the past revived in the present, is enrichingly evident also. The story of Shrewsbury is more than once recalled for continuity; Hotspur is movingly memorialized; Richard's fall is retold; the Coventry lists[5] whence the whole division arose are vividly conjured up; and the dying King summarizes his whole reign as 'a scene / Acting that argument' of conflict. The comic scenes also are as deeply involved in the past. The Hostess has known Falstaff these twenty-nine years, come peascod time;[6] old Double is dead, beloved of yore by John a Gaunt, but Jane Nightwork still lives though it is fifty-five year since she had Robin Nightwork by old Nightwork. Falstaff remembers Shallow's Clement's Inn days, and Shallow Falstaff when he was a crack not thus high. Time, its pressure in the present and future, its legacies from the past, is integral to the play, but not time as mere linear flow, time rather (through expectation and reminiscence) becoming the broad and intimate picture of the nation, opening out into that larger 'revolution of the times' in which all things are subject to Mutability, and giving life its larger context.

Life is not thereby humiliated. No play gives a richer sense of its reality. War and government with their plans, tavern-life with its humours, age with its ailments, local affairs run by such as Masters Tisick, Shallow, and Silence—trades, sports, songs, and dissipations, all form the variety of the ac-

---

4. *terminus ad quem* definite endpoint   5. *Coventry lists* combat ground enclosed by fortification   6. *peascod time* time when peas have pods

tion. Play-tags, military terms, ballad-snatches, Biblical fragments, and Homily echoes jostle references to shopkeepers'
satins, pewterers' hammers, brewers' buckets, the tilling of
land, the skills of archery, and caliver-management. Slang
and colloquialisms abound, the language of swaggerers,
catchpoles,[7] and whores. And what is seen and heard on the
stage affects us as the mere observable portion of an inex-
haustible circumambient life. . . .

Responsible moral standpoints great literature is expected
to have, and the *Henry IV*s are both great literature and related to, though transformed from, the morality tradition.
The problem is to get the morality substratum into balance
with the whole, in a response combining both judgment and
sympathy so as to be neither priggish nor sentimental. The
morality substratum gives the elements of guilt oppressed by
anxiety, hubris riding for a fall, youth choosing codes of conduct; but humanity itself gives that enriching cast of colour
whereby a mortal destiny broods above the doomed rebels
and the stricken King, the senile Justices, the tavern-
revellers, and the not-invulnerable Falstaff.

7. *catchpoles* a sheriff's officer, especially one who arrests debtors

The Warrior King in *Henry V*

Francis Fergusson

Francis Fergusson analyzes *Henry V* as a celebration of the hero who conquered French forces. Fergusson explains the play's major characters and episodes in light of that celebratory purpose. Francis Fergusson, theater director, educator, editor, and author of plays, poetry, and criticism, taught at Bennington College, Princeton University, Rutgers University, and Indiana University. He is the author of *Trope and Allegory: Themes Common to Dante and Shakespeare* and *The Idea of a Theatre: A Study of Ten Plays.*

This play is a celebration of the popular hero, "warlike Harry," and his famous victories in France. It has been severely criticized by devoted Shakespeareans, who object to the nationalistic pride which it expresses, and to the loose, fluent narrative style in which it is composed. But it has been a favorite in the theatre, and some of its passages of high rhetoric have become as familiar as proverbs. The best way to enjoy it is to see it on the stage, before a popular audience. Mr. Joseph Papp (who directed a superb production of it for the Shakespeare Festival in Central Park) has explained ... how absorbing it is when the producer relies on Shakespeare's theatre magic, which works in our time as it did in his.

Henry V, written in 1599, is in some respects a sequel to *Henry IV, Parts I and II.* In those plays we meet Henry as young Prince Hal, frequenter of taverns and companion of the great Falstaff and his disreputable friends. We meet the Prince's father, Henry IV, who had usurped the crown by the murder of Richard II, and dreams of leading a crusade to the Holy Land to expiate that crime. The shadow of his father's regicide still hangs over Henry V, and perhaps his "holy war" against France was undertaken in order to unify his people and to establish his own image as a religiously dedicated king. But *Henry V* is quite different from its predecessors. Henry had renounced the follies of his youth to assume the responsibilities of the crown, and in a famous scene in *Henry IV, Part II,* he had disowned his old friend Falstaff. When this play opens, Falstaff is dying offstage, and nothing matters but the conquest of France.

This focus upon the glories of war is unique in Shakespeare, and it makes *Henry V* quite unlike the other history plays. The historic sequence was essentially complete before *Henry V* was written. It recounts the bloody story of civil war from the murder of Richard II, when the War of the Roses began, to the accession of Henry VII, Queen Elizabeth's grandfather, who dethroned Richard III and at last pacified England. There is, of course, plenty of war treachery and private murder in the history plays, but that is never the point. The point is the quest for England's true welfare: peace, freedom, and order based on common loyalty to the crown. Shakespeare, following the chroniclers who had popularized that stretch of history, thought that the Tudors had finally established the crown upon a firm, just, and lasting basis. In the history plays he developed his rich, subtle vision of man, in society and in history, the vision which is most fully expressed in the great tragedies of his maturity.

Henry V adds nothing to this great theme, but one must suppose that Shakespeare, the most popular playwright in London, was all but obliged to devote a play to the warrior-king; he had, in fact, promised it in *Henry IV, Part II.* Henry plays a stellar role in Shakespeare's two main sources, Holinshed's *Chronicle,* and *The Famous Victories of Henry the Fifth,* an earlier play by an unknown author. The old play and the chroniclers had made Henry with his victories, into a familiar, exciting, popular legend, and it is that figure, symbol of England's military prowess, that Shakespeare recreates for his own theatre and acting company:

> O for a Muse of fire, that would ascend
> The brightest heaven of invention:
> A kingdom for a stage, princes to act,
> And monarchs to behold the swelling scene.
> Then would the warlike Harry, like himself,
> Assume the port of Mars, and at his heels,
> Leashed in like hounds, should Famine, Sword, and Fire
> Crouch for employment.
>
> (Prologue to I. 1–8)

We are gathered to celebrate once more Harry and his war, a patriotic ceremony, and the Chorus only hopes that the poet, his actors, and his stage will not disappoint the audience's expectations.

There is no difficulty in following the story of this play. Each act is based on a famous episode of Henry's career, and the Chorus with its superb verse-music maintains the martial mood and reminds us of the historic narrative that links the scenes. But in giving the audience the heroic legend that it demands, Shakespeare does not lose his own vision. He also presents a disillusioned picture of war itself, and that is why some critics think that his heart was not in this play. We can never know exactly what the play meant to Shakespeare or his audience; perhaps they relished it with more humor and irony than we usually give them credit for. But we can read the play with an eye to the contrasting effects—stirring, comic, cruel—which it has on a modern reader. And we can see . . . that it is all built to carry in the theatre.

THE CAUSES OF THE WAR WITH FRANCE

The first act is a prologue, for though the military motif is announced in the Chorus's very first words, we must go over the official "causes" of the war before the fighting can start. In Scene 1 the Archbishop of Canterbury and the Bishop of Ely candidly explain that they are offering Henry a great deal of money for his French War in order to induce him—not to say "bribe" him—to defend the Church from a bill that threatens to deprive it of most of its revenues. When Henry appears (Scene 2), he accepts the money, but also requires the Archbishop to justify his claim to the crown of France. The Archbishop obliges with a long, pedantic legal argument straight from Holinshed. Mr. Papp (as he explains) played this scene as comedy, and it is probable that Shakespeare intended it that way. No one could really follow the controversies about the Salic Law in the theatre; everyone wants Henry to get started; and in that situation the Archbishop's long-winded rationalizing is bound to seem laughably irrelevant.

But the Archbishop then proceeds to find Biblical sanction for the English cause, thus quieting Henry's conscience, and making the attack on France a kind of crusade. Henry's religious dedication was part of the legend, and it is stressed throughout the play. Moreover, the Archbishop gives an eloquent picture of the ideal monarchy, in which the swarming

diversity of human nature and purpose is united in obedience to the King:

> Therefore doth heaven divide
> The state of man in divers functions,
> Setting endeavour in continual motion;
> To which is fixed, as an aim or butt,[1]
> Obedience: for so work the honey-bees,
> Creatures that by a rule in nature teach
> The act of order to a peopled kingdom.
>
> (I.ii.183–89)

The whole speech is a carefully written and richly meta-
phorical exposition of Shakespeare's own sense of order,
both in human society and in the drama that reflects it. The
effect of the speech is to relate this play to the theme of the
histories, and to remind us that Henry, as King, is the symbol and custodian of England's moral well-being.

The act ends with a sharp turn from England's inner
order to the simpler motive of this play, foreign conquest;
when Henry receives the Dauphin's insulting gift of tennis
balls and makes his spirited reply, we can yell "Hurrah for
our side!" The Chorus, opening Act II, rejoices in this single-
minded drive:

> Now all the youth of England are on fire,
> And silken dalliance in the wardrobe lies.
> Now thrive the armourers, and honour's thought
> Reigns solely in the breast of every man.
>
> (Prologue II.1–4)

As the stage is peopled with characters of many kinds, in this
act and the next, we see that they are all focused on the warlike "aim or butt"; as the Archbishop puts it: "So may a thousand actions once afoot, / End in one purpose." The French,
as we see them at various stages of the campaign, are perforce sucked into the same motivation: "honor" and obedience to *their* King.

There is one more famous episode to be dealt with before
we embark: the conspiracy of Cambridge, Scroop and Grey,
who were bribed by the French, with their "pale policy," to
murder King Henry. Shakespeare presents it swiftly in Act II,
Scene 2. The treacherous plot increases our sympathy for
Henry, and therefore our war-fever, and when the conspirators repent on the way to their execution, the patriotic emotions acquire a new solemnity.

---

1. *butt* target

CONTRASTING THEMES IN THE INVASION STORY

In Acts II, III and IV the central story of Henry's invasion is accompanied by two contrasting themes: that of Falstaff's bedraggled old friends, and that of the British officers Gower, Fluellen, Macmorris and Jamy, who represent respectively the English, Welsh, Irish and Scottish soldiers that make up Henry's army.

Nym, Bardolph, Pistol and Nell Quickly appear in Act II, Scene 1, a sardonic contrast to the stirring Chorus that opens the act. Shakespeare's audience would have remembered them from *Henry IV* as the disreputable companions of Falstaff and of Henry himself when he was young Prince Hal. But now they are older and sadder, and we learn from them that Falstaff, that sweet monster, is dying. Nell says, "the King has killed his heart," thereby reminding us of the painful scene in *Henry IV, Part II,* when Henry disowns his old friend. When they return in Scene 3, Nell describes Falstaff's death in a speech which, with its mixture of pathos and humor, is worthy of Falstaff himself. This shameless crew is often thought of as comic relief, and it certainly does serve to deflate the pomposity of war with welcome laughter. Yet at the same time we see, through them, the meanest aspects of the army. Pistol's version of the war-motive is humorous, but the humor bites:

> Let us to France, like horse-leeches my boys,
> To suck, to suck, the very blood to suck.
>
> (II.iii.57–58)

As they appear throughout the play they always produce laughter with a somewhat bitter after-taste.

Gower, Fluellen, Macmorris and Jamy first appear in Act III, Scene 2, where they serve to put Pistol and his confederates in their place, and to counteract the impression they make. Shakespeare presents the racial types very much as popular fiction presents the racial types that make up our armies. He laughs affectionately at their accents and customs, while carefully demonstrating that they are all equally brave and equally loyal to the crown.

PREPARATIONS FOR BATTLE

It is in the scenes in the French Court and the French camp that we feel most strongly the jingoistic element in the play. We can only sympathize with King Charles when he receives Henry's impossible ultimatum (Act II, Scene 4), and endeavors to rouse his countrymen. But thereafter the silly Dauphin becomes the chief representative of the French side. And the closer we come to the battle of Agincourt, the climax of the play (Act IV), the more broadly does Shakespeare caricature the fopperies and vanities of the French.

In representing the great battle, Shakespeare diverts attention, as much as possible, away from the actual fighting,

---

THE BURDENS OF THE KING

In act 4, scene 1, on the eve of battle, Henry, alone in his tent, reflects on his kingly responsibilities and burdens.

"Upon the King! Let us our lives, our souls,
Our debts, our careful[1] wives,
Our children, and our sins, lay on the King!"
We must bear all. O hard condition,
Twin-born with greatness, subject to the breath[2]
Of every fool, whose sense no more can feel
But his own wringing![3] What infinite heart's-ease
Must kings neglect that private men enjoy!
And what have kings that privates have not too,
Save ceremony, save general ceremony?
And what art thou, thou idol Ceremony?
What kind of god art thou, that suffer'st more
Of mortal griefs than do thy worshippers?
What are thy rents? What are thy comings-in?
O Ceremony, show me but thy worth!
What is thy soul of adoration?[4]
Art thou aught else but place, degree, and form,[5]
Creating awe and fear in other men?
Wherein thou art less happy, being feared,
Than they in fearing.
What drink'st thou oft, instead of homage sweet,
But poisoned flattery? O, be sick, great greatness,
And bid thy ceremony give thee cure!
Thinks thou the fiery fever will go out
With titles blown[6] from adulation?
Will it give place to flexure[7] and low bending?
Canst thou, when thou command'st the beggar's knee,
Command the health of it? No, thou proud dream,
That play'st so subtely with a king's repose.

1. *careful* anxious   2. *breath* speech   3. *wringing* stomachache   4. *thy soul of adoration* the real nature of thy worship   5. *form* good order   6. *blown* inflated   7. *flexure* obsequious bowing

which, as the Chorus says, could hardly be adequately staged. And he has nothing to say about the military reasons for the extraordinary English victory. Holinshed carefully explains that the French relied on their heavily armed cavalry, while the English relied on their yeomen foot soldiers armed with longbows. The English archers got behind sharpened poles, on which the French horses foundered, and then let loose their showers of arrows. This battle, like Crécy,[2] still interests military historians, for it marks an important change in the composition of European armies: from the feudal knight to the yeoman foot soldier. But in accounting for the English victory, Shakespeare focuses entirely on the contrasting attitudes in the two armies: the arrogant overconfidence of the French, and the pious fortitude of the vastly outnumbered English.

Henry is, of course, the heart and soul of his army, and Shakespeare gives us, in Act III, superb images of the conquering hero. But at the same time he offers us (if we care to see them) absurd or horrifying glimpses of military bravura. Consider, for example, the opening sequence of Act III. The Chorus paints its exhilarating picture of the English Armada on its way:

Hear the shrill whistle, which doth order give
To sounds confused; behold the threaden sails,
Borne with th' invisible and creeping wind,
Draw the huge bottoms through the furrowed sea,

                                        (Prologue III.9–12)

and so brings us, with "the celerity of thought," to besieged Harfleur:

                        and the nimble gunner
With linstock now the devilish cannon touches,
                [Alarum, and chambers go off, within.]
And down goes all before them.

                                        (Prologue III.32–34)

Whereupon Henry himself rushes on to lead the charge, with that speech which countless actors and countless reciters in schools and colleges have made famous:

Once more unto the breach, dear friends, once more;
Or close the wall up with our English dead.

                                        (I.i.1–2)

The effect can be electrifying in the theatre, but if one reads

2. a northern French town where Edward III of England defeated Philip VI of France, a decisive battle in the Hundred Years' War fought on August 26, 1346

Henry's speech quietly one may notice how technically he induces the proper spirit in his men:

> Then imitate the action of the tiger;
> Stiffen the sinews, summon up the blood.
>
> (I.i.6–7)

Modern soldiers are (or were) taught pugnacity in a similar way: they had to grunt savagely as they pushed their bayonets into the sandbags that represented the enemy. When red-nosed Bardolph charges in at the head of his ragamuffins immediately after Henry's charge, yelling, "On, on, on, on, on, to the breach, to the breach, to the breach!" he can hardly fail to bring down the house. When we next see Henry, he is forcing the citizens of Harfleur to open their gates by reminding them of the fate of a sacked town:

> What rein can hold licentious wickedness,
> When down the hill he holds his fierce career?
>
> (III.iii.22–23)

We see him as a swift, relentless invader who nevertheless offers mercy if the enemy will yield. But his speech also reminds us vividly of the mischief his war has let loose.

HENRY THE WARRIOR

Shakespeare builds his most careful picture of Henry as the religiously dedicated warrior in Act IV, Scene 1, the night before Agincourt. The Chorus sets the scene on the eve of battle:

> Now entertain conjecture³ of a time,
> When creeping murmur and the poring⁴ dark
> Fills the wide vessel of the universe.
> From camp to camp, through the foul womb of night
> The hum of either army stilly⁵ sounds.
>
> (Prologue iv.1–5)

The French are waiting eagerly, in their thousands; the English are few and starving, but Henry restores their courage with "A little touch of Harry in the night":

> That every wretch, pining and pale before,
> Beholding him, plucks comfort from his looks.
>
> (Prologue iv.41–42)

Disguised as a soldier "under Sir Thomas Erpingham" Henry meets Bates and Williams, who proves to be a tough-minded critic of the whole war. Williams wants to know how

---

3. *entertain conjecture* imagine   4. *poring* peering   5. *stilly* in the still night

such slaughter can be justified; how he and other common soldiers can know whether the English cause is righteous or not; how the King can possibly take responsibility for so much suffering: just such questions as must torment any soldier as he waits for the carnage to begin. Henry tries to discuss these hard matters reasonably with Williams, and they agree on the necessity of obedience to the commander, without which an army (or any common enterprise) is impossible. But Williams insists that the King has the best of it, and he and Henry both lose their tempers. They postpone their quarrel until after the battle, when we shall see it patched up as well as possible under the circumstances (Act IV, Scenes 7 and 8).

Henry and Williams elide the question of the justice of their cause. We like to think that every soldier should know why he is fighting; but Henry and Williams seem to agree that a common soldier cannot be expected to know and correctly judge the causes of the war; they leave that to the King. We have seen that Henry, as King, had left it to the Archbishop of Canterbury (Act I, Scene 2). Thus, if we care to think about it, we may see King and soldier alike risking their lives in the faith, certified by the Church, that they are obeying the will of God. But at this point we are not given much time to think; the fatal night is near its end, Henry and all his men are in mortal peril. When Henry, left alone, meditates on the intolerable burden of rule, it is impossible not to sympathize with his human plight. And it seems natural, after he has bade old Erpingham good night, that he should resort to prayer (end of Scene 1). Henry's religious faith is stressed again after the battle, when it is badly needed to explain (if not justify) the horrors of Agincourt. We have by that time seen Henry order his soldiers to murder their prisoners (Scene 6). We have heard that the French slaughtered the helpless English boys who were left with the baggage (Scene 7). We have heard the amazing statistics of death and destruction (Scene 8); but Henry attributes his almost incredible victory to God, and orders that prayers of thanksgiving be offered and the dead properly buried.

Agincourt was Henry's most famous victory, but the war dragged on for years, and France was "lost" in the disastrous reign of Henry VI. The readers of the popular *Chronicles* in Shakespeare's audience knew this very well, and the Chorus alludes to the facts before Act V and in the Epilogue, but only to dismiss them. The fifth act is based on Henry's betrothal to Princess Katharine, which triumphantly ends that phase of the war.

THE WOOING OF KATHARINE

Act V has been sharply criticized by many authorities, including the great Dr. Johnson who thought that Shakespeare had used up his material in Act IV and was obliged to add the wooing scene to fill out the evening. But we can see, I think, that the wooing of Katharine is the natural ending for the play as Shakespeare very knowingly planned it. Having seen our idol in action, winning against great odds, we want a glimpse of him after his victory, like a baseball player in the locker-room after the big game, kissing his wife and bashfully accepting congratulations. We see Henry with Katharine in just such a relaxed and endearing mood, a surprisingly clumsy lover, a plainspoken, simple Englishman after all (Scene 2). Like so much comedy, this scene plays far better than it reads; with an attractive and skillful Katharine, it may be charming in the theatre. It makes us forget the bitterness of war and, like the traditional happy ending of comedy, sends us home content with the evening's entertainment.

It is evident that the Henry of this scene is not the subtle young man we know as Prince Hal in *Henry IV, Part I*. It is open to question whether he is consistent with Henry the conqueror, and Henry the pious king, whom we meet in the first parts of this play. . . .

In constructing his play about warlike Harry for his popular audience, Shakespeare (being the poet he was) could not follow his predecessors very closely. . . . He had created the marvelously unwarlike Falstaff; he was probably already working on *Hamlet* (1600); and when he considered war, he saw a great deal besides the splendor of heroism. Nevertheless he made the play an evocation of the English fighting spirit which has served his countrymen as a sort of patriotic ceremony from that day to this, especially when (as in World War II) their country has been in danger. His theatre magic and his grasp of popular psychology is so sure that a good production of *Henry V* can be a moving experience for us, also.

Perspective in *Henry V*

John Russell Brown

John Russell Brown argues that in *Henry V* Shakespeare shifts from broad to narrow perspectives,
with Henry always at the center. The first part of the
play is panoramic, using the techniques of the
chorus, minor characters, and contrasting settings.
The focus then shifts narrowly to Henry and his
personal feelings in the scenes before the battle.
Finally a broad view is reestablished once victory
has been attained. John Russell Brown has taught
English at the University of Birmingham, the University of Sussex, and the University of Michigan and
directed the Orbit Theatre Company. He is the author
of *Shakespeare and His Comedies* and *Shakespeare:
The Tragedy of Macbeth* and an editor of *Henry V*.

In the theater *Henry the Fifth* is renowned for its pageantry,
battles and crowd scenes, its varied collection of minor characters, and the unquestioned dominance of its hero. . . .

Written in 1599, a year or so before *Hamlet, Henry the
Fifth* was Shakespeare's last history play for ten years or
more, and he appears to have taken no risks. Despite its
crowd scenes and wide range of characters, it has a simple
plot of wars, a battle and a peace, centered on its undoubted
hero. A Chorus, before each act, encourages the audience's
warmest responses, and invites its imagination to see two
mighty monarchies, and follow Harry as a type of virtue,
"the mirror of all Christian kings." For most of the play, the
King appears publicly, in ceremonial consultation or address, or as leader of his army; his words are well-ordered,
and clearly and fully understood. When he surprises the
French ambassador with defiance or the three traitors with
a knowledge of their crimes, the audience has been prepared in advance so that its understanding suffers no shock.
The minor characters are all dependent on Harry and yet

make only occasional appearances in unconsecutive scenes, usually without the hero, so that the independent plot-interest they awaken is both small and quickly answered. Except for the French royal house, none already established has a place in the last long scene; but two entirely new characters are then introduced to eminence, Isabel and the Duke of Burgundy. The play's structure is firmly centered; its setting splendid, varied, broad. In its sweeping, general impression, and usually in performance, *Henry the Fifth* is a popular pageant play of the "star of England," and incidentally of his people and his victories. . . .

ACTS I AND II SHARPEN THE FOCUS ON THE HERO PLACED IN A WIDE VIEW

The Chorus is at hand to keep the picture fully animated and expectation forward, with:

> Now all the youth of England are on fire,
> And silken dalliance[1] in the wardrobe lies.
>
> (Prologue II.1–2)

So the predominant focus is maintained, a wide view of a pageant narrative.

But even the first act is not superficial. Because Shakespeare has not sharpened the focus by his usual devices as he could so effectively have done, this needs to be especially noticed. The audience's appreciation is quickened without bringing the hero closely and intimately to its attention; there is no soliloquy, no aside, no self-conscious or nervous speech, no sudden, unprepared exit or utterance, or transition of mood. The audience's view is centered on Harry and its perception is acute, but Harry is always the central figure of a group, and the audience knows him in the same kind of terms as it knows the other characters.

The second act, like the first, gives no occasion for an intense focus on Harry, but Shakespeare has ensured still greater clarity, and more deeply questioning responses. Among the noisy quarrels of Pistol and his fellows comes news that Falstaff is sick and broken in heart after Harry has banished him; and this, in turn, is followed by the contrasting affirmation, "The King is a good king . . . it must be as it may . . . lambkins, we will live"; here the audience cannot give one simple emotional response. Then Harry in public

---

1. *silken dalliance* silken clothes suitable for flirtation

discloses the treachery of three friends, elaborating formally
on the evil hearts under their apparent goodness:

>   thy fall hath left a kind of blot
> To mark the full-fraught man and best indued
> With some suspicion.

(II.ii.138–40)

The audience is being made aware that the wide scene can
be viewed in more than one way. Harry himself may be
moved, for before pronouncing judgment he speaks a short
sentence:

>   I will weep for thee;
> For this revolt of thine, methinks, is like
> Another fall of man.

(II.ii.140–42)

This is not a clear intensification of the focus in a deeply revealing soliloquy, for the words are spoken formally for all
to hear; but it makes sure that any questioning aroused by
this incident may touch Harry as well as others. Then he
concludes the scene securely, with a final conciseness that
is habitual to him:

>   . . . let us deliver
> Our puissance into the hand of God,
> Putting it straight in expedition.[2]
> Cheerly to sea; the signs[3] of war advance:
> No king of England, if not King of France!

(II.ii.189–93)

But now even this does not remain simple: Harry's confident
committal into the "hand of God" is followed by the hostess'
reflective account of Falstaff fumbling with the sheets and
playing with flowers, and crying out "God, God, God!" three
or four times:

> Now I, to comfort him, bid him 'a should not think of God; I
> hoped there was no need to trouble himself with any such
> thoughts yet. So 'a bade me lay more clothes on his feet.

(II.iii.20ff.)

Harry went to France asserting that he went hand in hand
with God; Falstaff is said to have gone "away and it had been
any christom child"; and then Pistol leaves to follow the King:

> Let us to France, like horse-leeches, my boys,
> To suck, to suck, the very blood to suck!

(II.iii.57–58)

Contrasts sharpen the wide view; and some of the audience,

---

2. *expedition* motion   3. *signs* standards

if they stopped to consider, would think they knew more of the overall issues than any one of the dramatis personae.

Bickering at the French Court, differences among Harry's soldiers, the charm, absurdity and prim bawdiness of the French Princess learning English, all may cause the audience to question, in a general way, the motives and comprehension of the characters. And Harry's invocation of the "fleshed soldier, rough and hard of heart... With conscience wide as hell" as a threat to Harfleur, may heighten its sense of what is involved and cause it to question Harry's attitude to the brutality he is prepared to encourage. Then, as the battle of Agincourt approaches, his reply to Montjoy, the French Herald, shows all his earlier resource—vaunting wit, pride, modest self-blame, confidence in God, unhesitating threat of carnage, concise utterance. Expectation for the crisis of the action is heightened and wide, but in a new manner "objective" or watchful. The audience has seen more aspects of each figure in the picture than those figures seem to have seen themselves.

PREPARATION FOR BATTLE

Yet the battle is prepared for in leisurely manner. The Chorus describes its setting with careful artistry, as in the multiple epithets of "cripple tardy-gaited night," or the Spenserian prettiness of "paly flames." Then Harry, disguised in a great cloak, wanders alone, meeting his various soldiers. He is no longer attended as a king, and speaking as a man in isolation he comes closer to the audience. Two very brief soliloquies are his first in the play. Then, talking to Williams, a tendentious, "ordinary" soldier, he considers the responsibility for life and death and deeds in a new vein:

> some (peradventure) have on them the guilt of premeditated and contrived murder; some, of beguiling virgins... some, making the wars their bulwark, that have before gored the gentle bosom of peace with pillage and robbery. Now, if these men have defeated the law and outrun native punishment,[4] though they can outstrip men, they have no wings to fly from God.
>
> (IV.i.165–73)

... Despite its length, Harry's meditative, elaborating prose has the conviction to keep Williams silent until its conclusion, when his only comment is simple agreement. For the audience, the unusual lack of concision, meter and pace gives

4. *outrun ... punishment* escaped punishment at home

Harry a new voice, helping to realize the new range of his
thought and feeling which may well embody some of their
own incipient comments on the action. As the soldiers move
off and Harry is alone, the dramatic focus will be, for the first
time, potentially intense and deep. There follows a questioning, yet formal, consideration of the cares of kingship, and a
lyrical, yet still formal, consideration of a peasant's laboring
life. This is yet another aspect of Harry's response, but he
seems to shape his thoughts consciously and concludes as if
presenting another concise summing-up in public. When Erpingham enters to call him to battle, the widest view seems
about to be reestablished. But this valued messenger is sent
away and Harry falls on his knees and prays:

> O God of battles, steel my soldiers' hearts.

> (IV.i.307)

He knows their weakness:

> Possess them not with fear! Take from them now
> The sense of reck'ning, or th' opposèd numbers
> Pluck their hearts from them.

> (IV.i.308–10)

Then he speaks of himself, urgently, repetitively, impul-
sively. He mentions precisely a fear which hitherto has not
been made an issue anywhere on the surface of the drama:

> Not today, O Lord,
> O, not today, think not upon the fault
> My father made in compassing the crown!
> I Richard's body have interrèd new,
> And on it have bestowed more contrite tears
> Than from it issued forcèd drops of blood.
> Five hundred poor I have in yearly pay.

> (IV.i.309–15)

The expression of purpose—"to pardon blood"—is empha-
sized by word order and by meter, and twice the lines break
before their end, to give urgency and weight to a new idea:

> Five hundred poor I have in yearly pay,
> Who twice a day their withered hands hold up
> Toward heaven, to pardon blood;
> And I have built two chantries,[5]
> Where the sad and solemn priests sing still[6]
> For Richard's soul. More will I do:
> Though all that I can do is nothing worth;
> Since that my penitence comes after all,
> Imploring pardon.

> (IV.i.315–23)

5. *chantries* chapels where priests sing masses for the repose of the souls of the dead
6. *still* continuously

There is a half-line pause, then Gloucester enters and Harry is once more the leader, assured and ready:

> *Gloucester.* My liege!
> *King.* My brother Gloucester's voice? Ay.
>   I know thy errand; I will go with thee.
>   The day, my friends, and all things stay for me.
>   (IV.i.323–26)

This sequence has shown Harry as king, son and man, conscious of his responsibility and that of other men in war as in peace, and acknowledging a fear within himself, an awareness that, though he may outstrip the judgment of men, he has "no wings to fly from God." As he prepares for battle a short moment of intense focus has revealed his inmost secrets, and his knowledge that no human help can redress the past. . . .

HARRY'S CONCERN FOR HONOR AND AN HONEST HEART

Harry had perhaps wept for the traitors as they reminded him that a "full-fraught" man may be suspected. He had earnestly commanded the archbishop to justify his title to the French crown with

>   conscience washed
>   As pure as sin with baptism.
>   (I.ii.31–32)

Moreover, the need for an honest heart and Harry's equal responsibility with all men are taken up in the following scenes in ways which can betray to the audience's intensified interest his deep concern with these issues.

His address to the soldiers before battle is not a spurring on of others, in the vein of "Once more unto the breach, dear friends, once more." Compared with that conjuring up of the blood before Harfleur, it is thoughtful:

>   . . . if it be a sin to covet honor,
>   I am the most offending soul alive.
>   (IV.iii.28–29)

. . . Harry covets honor in his heart and would have his soldiers do so with him; and this is his battle cry. In fight he is still valiant, gay almost with hardiness, angry, ruthless, efficient. He is again the Harry of the first three acts, ready in anger to kill all his prisoners. But afterwards there are further reminders of his inward knowledge and need. Perhaps the repeated insistence with which he gives all credit to God is one. Certainly when Fluellen, the robustly confident

Welshman, claims brotherhood—

> I am your Majesty's countryman, I care not who know it. . . .
> I need not to be ashamed of your Majesty, praised be God, so
> long as your Majesty is an honest man—

> (IV.vii.114–18)

Harry answers directly and simply, "God keep me so"—that
is an "honest man"—and only then turns to public, urgent
matters. Later, when Williams excuses his quarrel, his
words must strike the monarch more deeply than the puzzled soldier could guess:

> All offenses, my lord, come from the heart: never came any
> from mine that might offend your Majesty.

> (IV.viii.46–48)

Some of the audience, at least, will remember that this king
has recognized an "offending" heart within himself. . . .

THE WIDE VIEW REESTABLISHED

In that *Henry the Fifth* has a central scene of intense focus
which shows the King acknowledging his guilt, it is obviously indebted to *Henry the Fourth, Part Two*. But Shakespeare has modified his purpose and his technique. Harry
does not win peace like his father, only a recognition of the
need for pardon; moreover, he remains a figure in the center of others. In this play, the predominantly wide view is
reestablished and the audience's inward knowledge of
Harry's personal crisis is used to deepen the view of the
whole scene, and of the many other characters to whom, unlike Henry the Fourth, this king is dramatically related.
Williams, Fluellen, Montjoy, and the soldiers are only the
first to reenter the picture; the whole fifth act sustains and
develops this experience.

It begins with the ludicrous unmasking of the braggart,
Pistol, who is forced to eat Fluellen's leek. This is more than
a comic counterpart to heroism, for he is left alone onstage
and in a direct and immediate soliloquy he may briefly pro-
voke empathetic sympathy:

> Old I do wax, and from my weary limbs
> Honor is cudgeled.

> (V.i.87–88)

The moment is passed as he gathers confidence and decides
to return to England to cheat and steal. And the audience's
view is fully extended as the kings of France and England
and their nobility fill the stage for the final scene in quiet

and formal meeting. In a long, deliberate speech, the peace-maker, the Duke of Burgundy, describes France ravaged by war and a generation of her sons growing

> like savages—as soldiers will,
> That nothing do but meditate on blood—
>
> (V.ii.59–60)

The whole play, its action and consequences, passes in general review, seen this time with French eyes—or rather with a timeless concern with the arts and sciences of peace, and with natural affections. This new perspective is generalized, but as the two parties leave the stage to debate the terms of peace, Harry remains with Katharine, Princess of France, and her maid: here the dramatic interest is as narrow as before Agincourt.

HARRY WOOS KATHARINE

As Harry woos his bride, he speaks sometimes as if in soliloquy, for she cannot understand all he says. It is a complex scene: clearly this is to be a political, but also a personally felt, marriage; clearly Harry offers himself as a simple man, but he does so with wit and eloquence; clearly he is confident and a conqueror, but he is also suitor. And as he warms to his theme he speaks again, directly and with immediacy, of a "good heart":

> a good leg will fall, a straight back will stoop, a black beard will turn white, a curled pate will grow bald, a fair face will wither, a full eye will wax hollow: but a good heart, Kate, is the sun and the moon, or rather, the sun, and not the moon, for it shines bright and never changes, but keeps his course truly.
>
> (V.ii.166–71)

Katharine questions "Is it possible dat I sould love de ennemie of France?" And he can only answer with a riddle:

> No, it is not possible . . . but in loving me you should love the friend of France: for I love France so well, that I will not part with a village of it—I will have it all mine. And, Kate, when France is mine and I am yours, then yours is France, and you are mine.
>
> (V.ii.181–85)

He gets the deserved response: "I cannot tell wat is dat," and the plain soldier is forced to attempt "false French." Yet now they speak more freely, and as Harry's blood "begins to flatter" him that he is loved, he speaks lightly of his father's ambition, which had held him in prayer before battle:

Now beshrew[7] my father's ambition! He was thinking of civil
wars when he got[8] me, therefore was I created with a stub-
born outside, with an aspect of iron, that when I come to woo
ladies, I fright them.

(V.ii.241–44)

Too much should not be made of this reference; it shows a
relaxation of mind, not a conscious change of attitude. Soon,
against the "custom" of France, they kiss, and are silent together. And then, gently and with an intimate, relaxing jest,
Harry acknowledges what has been given and taken, and
understood without words:

You have witchcraft in your lips, Kate: there is more eloquence in a sugar touch of them than in the tongues of the
French Council . . .

(V.ii.300–303)

The stage fills again, the relaxed mood being sustained by
Burgundy's heavy teasing of the bridegroom. The latter still
insists on receiving the cities of the bride's dowry and the
title of Inheritor of France, but with a general "Amen," the
contesting sides stand solemnly side by side in agreement.
As the focus thus widens fully again, and steadies, there is
another silence as Harry kisses Kate before them all, as his
"sovereign Queen." But the view is also acute and questioning. Shakespeare has not attempted to show a love match, or
a union in which the audience may be easily confident; and
now the bride's mother reminds them frankly of

. . . fell[9] jealousy
Which troubles oft the bed of blessed marriage.

(V.ii.391–92)

The long wooing scene—far more elaborate than at first
seems to be required by the dramatic context—has served to
show afresh and with an intermittent intensity the need for
an honest heart, and the danger and embarrassment of rely-
ing on words alone; and, in the kiss, it suggested an inward
understanding, peace, affection, unity that is a greater sol-
vent, a more powerful reorganizing power, than words or
battles: the silence of the kiss is a shared silence in which
the audience instinctively participates.

Representatives of two societies take up, with remem-
brances of past action and hopes and prayers for the future,
their final positions of concord; and Harry, speaking formally within the wide picture, closes the play with a further

7. *beshrew* plague on   8. *got* begot   9. *fell* fierce

pointer to the heart of all matters:

> . . . we'll take your oath,
> And all the peers', for surety[10] of our leagues.
> Then shall I swear to Kate, and you to me,
> *And may our oaths well kept and prosp'rous be!*[11]
>
> (V.ii.399–402)

Shakespeare has finished his long series of history plays by presenting a group of people standing together: behind appearances and oaths there is need for an "honest heart"; within the wide range, the audience is invited to search for signs of inward peace, good faith, affection, trust, of that which "never changes, but keeps his course truly." When the stage empties and the Chorus announces the end of the action, he also speaks of later times when all France was lost and England bled again. If this play has received its intended "acceptance," it will not be destructive or irrelevant to remind the audience that the final, peaceful grouping was neither fully honest nor fully permanent.

Henry the Fifth is a hero-centered historical pageant that presents a clear narrative and varied characters. In that, it differs from Shakespeare's earlier histories, with their concern with political necessity or "commodity," with rebellion, power and conscience, and with God's providence. But it was not an easy, or routine, declension from a more serious drama. The play tries to relate the personal, instinctive and affectionate truth of human relationships, exemplified in the acceptance of Kate and Harry, with warfare, politics and national rivalries; and it has effected this in the wide range of characters that is such an important aid to the full acceptance of this play. Mistress Quickly's account of Falstaff's death, Fluellen's incongruous loyalty and familiarity with his king, Williams' defense of his honest heart, Pistol's recognition of the end of his campaign, and Kate and Harry's kiss, all represent the necessary element of human understanding, as eloquent as Burgundy's general evocation of the virtues of peace. The audience's involvement in these moments is of a different nature from its involvement in the narrative of war and politics, and is of pervasive, because unthinking, importance in the reception of the play as a whole.

---

10. *surety* ratification   11. editor's italics

CHAPTER 4

The Lesser-Known History Plays

READINGS ON
THE HISTORIES

Shakespeare's First Plays: 1, 2, and *3 Henry VI*

Clifford Leech

Clifford Leech explains what is known concerning the authorship and chronology of Shakespeare's first plays, *1, 2,* and *3 Henry VI*. In addition, Leech summarizes the episodes of Part 1 and the plots of Parts 2 and 3. Clifford Leech has taught English at the University of Toronto in Canada. He has also been a research fellow at the Shakespearian Folger Library in Washington, D.C., and is the author of *Shakespeare's Tragedies and Other Studies in Seventeenth-Century Drama.*

It is impossible to discuss the *Henry VI* plays without referring first to the problems of authorship and chronology. They were published together in the Folio of 1623, but, although this is the first occasion of the printing of Part I, the other two Parts had appeared long before in corrupt versions. In 1594 there was published a quarto volume with the title *The First part of the Contention betwixt the two famous Houses of Yorke and Lancaster,* and in 1595 an octavo with the title *The true Tragedie of Richard Duke of Yorke.* These two texts were published together as *The Whole Contention betweene the two Famous Houses, Lancaster and Yorke* in 1619. There is thus a strong bibliographical link between Parts II and III. There is a link, too, in subject-matter. These two Parts present a continuous narrative from the King's marriage with the French princess Margaret to the murder of Henry VI and the establishment on the throne of the Yorkist Edward IV. Part I, on the other hand, is principally concerned with the wars in France at the beginning of Henry VI's reign, although it also includes the beginning of the York-Lancaster opposition, the planning of Henry's marriage to Margaret, and a number of incidents that historically

Reprinted from *William Shakespeare: The Chronicles,* by Clifford Leech (London: Longmans, Green & Co., 1962).

were later than some that occur in Part II.

There is a good case for assuming that Part I was a play acted by Strange's Men,[1] for Henslowe's[2] *Diary* records their performance of *Harey the vj* as a new play in March 1592, and in the same year Thomas Nashe[3] in *Pierce Pennilesse* refers to the current acting of a play in which Talbot's military triumphs were displayed: as *1 Henry VI* has Talbot's campaigns as one of its chief concerns, we can reasonably identify the play in the 1623 Folio with the play referred to by Henslowe and Nashe. Yet Part III must have been written by September 1592, for Robert Greene[4] parodies a line from it in his death-bed tract *Greenes Groats-worth of Witte.* And Part III (doubtless with Part II, for the two can hardly be separated) was, according to the title-page of the 1595 edition, acted by Pembroke's Men.[5]

SHAKESPEARE'S CONTRIBUTION

There has been much discussion of the extent of Shakespeare's contribution to the three Parts. Edmund Malone believed that the publications of 1594 and 1595 were source plays re-written by Shakespeare as 2 and 3 *Henry VI,* and that this had occasioned the attack on Shakespeare in *Greenes Groats-worth of Witte,* where he is described as 'an upstart Crow, beautified with our feathers'. Now, however, critic Peter Alexander has won almost universal support for his view that *The First part of the Contention* and *The true Tragedie* are 'bad quartos', i.e. texts derivative from the plays now known as 2 and 3 *Henry VI* but contaminated through memorial transmission. There is still disagreement concerning the extent to which we can find Shakespeare's hand in the three Parts and concerning the order in which they were written. There will probably always be speculation on these matters, but the present weight of opinion is on the side of recognizing a much larger Shakespearian element in the 'trilogy' than was formerly the case. Although no certainty is possible, it seems likely that Shakespeare wrote a two-part play on the Wars of the Roses for Pembroke's Men, and that the play recorded by Henslowe as *Harey the vj* was adapted by him when, in 1594, he joined the newly-formed Lord

---

1. actors at the Rose Theater   2. Philip Henslowe, of the Rose and other theaters   3. critic, satirist, and playwright during Shakespeare's time   4. author of pamphlets, romances, and plays; may have shared authorship of the original *Henry VI* plays   5. a company of actors

Chamberlain's Men along with some of the actors who had belonged to Strange's. In this way a trilogy was put together out of an original two-part Shakespearian play and a play (originally non-Shakespearian) that concentrated on the earliest events of Henry VI's reign. It may well be that Part I was written later than Parts II and III, but was made into a forepiece for the other two plays when Shakespeare revised it.

If this line of speculation is followed, we must regard Part I as only partially Shakespeare's and Parts II and III as mainly, if not wholly, his. And that will fit our response to the plays as dramatic achievements. Those who saw the Birmingham Repertory Theatre's performances of the three Parts in 1951–53 are likely to hold a more favourable view of their quality than was formerly common. Nevertheless, there can be no doubt that a higher level is reached in Parts II and III than in Part I.

A SHAPELESS PIECE OF WRITING

In view of the theory of composition and authorship here suggested, we need not linger for more than a moment with Part I. It is a fairly shapeless piece of writing, beginning with some pomp and indeed impressiveness with the funeral of Henry V, where the Lancastrian nobles are quickly at odds, but soon falling into an anecdotal kind of drama in which incidents are presented in turn for the sake of immediate dramatic effect rather than for their contribution to a total pattern. An extreme example of this is the introduction of a French Countess who plans to murder Talbot by inviting him to her castle. Talbot shows his shrewdness by accepting the invitation but ensuring that his troops are in reach when the Countess shows her hand. The incident has no effect on later action: it is a mere anecdote of the war. Nevertheless, there is vigorous drama in the opposition between the Lord Protector, Humphrey of Gloucester, and the Bishop of Winchester, in the display of Talbot's prowess and his bravery in death, in the crude but lively portrayal of Joan of Arc, and in the first indications of Richard Plantagenet's rise to a position of importance in the kingdom. Concerning this last strand in the play, there is common consent that Shakespeare wrote the Temple Garden scene, where Plantagenet and the Earl of Somerset, having quarrelled in the Temple hall about a point of law (we are never told what it is), pluck respectively a white and a red rose and invite those who support them to do likewise. This scene, for which the sixteenth-century chronicles provide no source, most dramatically presages the state of open conflict between York and Lancaster.

The French wars of Henry VI's reign were hardly to be seen as a reason for national pride, but the author of *1 Henry VI* did what he could to make them palatable. He put considerable stress on the achievements of Talbot, he presented Joan as a witch and a wanton, and he ended the play, quite unhistorically, with peace terms that declare the French King to be a viceroy under Henry VI, paying tribute to England: Professor Dover Wilson has pointed out that these terms are derived from those offered to, and rejected by, the French in 1435.

THE STORY OF PARTS II AND III

Parts II and III tell a continuous and wide-ranging story. For spectators it cannot be easy to grasp the exact relationships between the main characters and the genealogical details that made it possible for Richard Plantagenet, now Duke of York, to lay claim to the throne. For that reason, in Act II scene ii of Part II, the author inserted a scene in which York, addressing the Earl of Salisbury and his son the Earl of Warwick, gives a full account of the ancestry of both himself and Henry VI. The scene is not great drama, but it was necessary if the audience were to see the grounds for the dynastic quarrel. . . . The action of the two plays is widely spread through England, with a short excursion into France in Part III, and the dramatist has clearly wanted to bring home to his audience the sense of a civil war ranging destructively over the country. For non-English readers, in particular, the many references to place-names may be confusing and will certainly not have the impact that was intended in the writing. . . .

A DIFFERENT MATERIAL AND STRUCTURE

Part II differs from Part III in material and consequently in structure. Open war between York and Lancaster does not begin until Part II is almost over, and the greater part of the play is concerned with the gradual development of York's plans, with his waiting until Humphrey Duke of Gloucester is dead (helping modestly in his downfall), and with the enmities stirred up by Henry's Queen Margaret. Departing from his sources, for in fact Margaret did not come to England until after the Duchess of Gloucester's disgrace, the author has made dramatic capital out of a rivalry between the Queen and the wife of the Lord Protector. In addition, he gives the audience a thrill of horror in showing the Duchess of

THE ENGLAND OF HENRY VI

Many important characters in Shakespeare's histories are known both by given name and by their royal titles' place names (e.g., Richard, duke of Gloucester, is often simply Gloucester). The map of England identifies these key places.

Gloucester using witchcraft in order to pry into the future, where she sees herself as England's Queen, and another thrill when Cardinal Beaufort dies in terror for his guilt in the killing of Gloucester. We have, too, a host of small incidents which, like the story of the Countess in Part I, can be regarded as dramatic anecdotes. There is the presence of Simpcox that he has been miraculously cured of blindness—a 'miracle' quickly exposed by Humphrey of Gloucester. There is the grim comedy of Horner, an armourer, and his man Peter. The man accuses his master of speaking in favour of York's title to the crown. The issue is put to trial by combat between these two men who are quite unfitted to the test. Peter is terrified, but the armourer comes drunk to the contest and is killed. There is the execution of the Earl of Suffolk, who is captured by pirates when he has been banished from England: they refuse to accept ransom for him because of his opposition to Gloucester and to York and his consorting with Margaret. Yet, unlike the Countess story in Part I, these incidents all play their parts in the economy of the play. The exposure of the Simpcox 'miracle' exhibits the shrewdness and commonsense of Gloucester, so badly needed in the England of Henry VI. The affair of Horner and Peter displays the common people taking part in the nobles' quarrel about the royal title, as does the killing of Suffolk by men who are pirates but claim to be concerned for England's welfare. Moreover, the formal combat between the armourer and his man is a parody of chivalric encounter: in a way remarkably sophisticated for this early drama, it implies a critical attitude towards the warring nobles whose quarrels are grotesquely mirrored in this fight between two simple men, one terrified, one drunk.

This use of a mirror-image appears more fully in the scenes towards the end of Part II showing Jack Cade's rebellion. In Act III York is made regent of Ireland. This, he tells us in soliloquy, will give him his opportunity, for he will have an army at his disposal in Ireland. He is encouraging the 'headstrong Kentishman' Jack Cade to rebel, under the pretence that he is descended from the Mortimers from whom York himself derives his claim to the throne. From Cade's degree of success York will be able to see how the country is affected to the Yorkist claim. Whatever happens, York can come from Ireland with his army and reap the harvest that Cade's rebellion has prepared for him. The greater part of Act IV is taken up with Cade's rebellion. It is a revolt of common men against nobility, of ignorance against learning, of nonsense against sense: it presents a vision of anarchy in which a man can be put to death for being able to read, in which savagery is unchecked by any accepted code of manners, in which the rebels foolishly dream that by a mere proclamation they can refashion the country according to their hearts' desire. It is not a pleasant picture of a mob at work that Shakespeare gives us here, but we should note that some of Cade's followers can, in their asides, make fun of him, and that York's speech in Act III makes it clear that the Kentishman has been deluded by an ambitious noble. Moreover, the anarchy into which London is plunged when Cade is briefly lord of the city is an anticipation of the state of the whole country when the nobles' quarrel comes fully into the open and a whole series of battles is fought between York and Lancaster. The armourer Horner spoke treason on York's behalf and was killed for it. Cade sets himself up as a Mortimer, and having killed London citizens and a noble or two, is deserted by his followers and is himself killed as a fugitive. He provides the occasion for York to bring his army from Ireland, under the pretence that he has come to put down Cade (now defeated). The small revolt of ignorant men is a prelude and a mirror for the larger and much crueller contest between their superiors in the realm. With this in mind, we shall not see Shakespeare here as primarily concerned with the mob's folly and barbarity: rather, he recognizes the nature of an armed mob, but sees in it an image of what civilized men can be when their weapons too are out.

This Second Part gains in strength as it proceeds. When battle has been joined in Act V, the Lancastrian Old Clifford is killed by York and the dead body is found by his son, Young Clifford. The character of this son is to be important in Part III, representing an extreme of Lancastrian ruthlessness. Here he addresses his father in words that usher in the grim slaughter of the Third Part:

> O, let the vile world end
> And the premised[6] flames of the last day
> Knit earth and heaven together!
> Now let the general trumpet blow his blast,
> Particularities[7] and petty sounds
> To cease! Wast thou ordain'd, dear father,

6. *premised* foreordained   7. *particularities* trifles

To lose thy youth in peace and to achieve
The silver livery of advised[8] age,
And in thy reverence and thy chair-days[9] thus
To die in ruffian battle? Even at this sight
My heart is turn'd to stone; and while 'tis mine
It shall be stony. York not our old men spares;
No more will I their babes. Tears virginal[10]
Shall be to me even as the dew to fire
And beauty, that the tyrant oft reclaims,[11]
Shall to my flaming wrath be oil and flax.
Henceforth I will not have to do with pity.

(V.ii.40–56)

The balancing of the grand generalities of the Last Judge-
ment in the first six lines with the intimate picture of Old
Clifford, murdered in 'ruffian battle' at a time poignantly described as his 'chair-days', and then the severity of the reso-
lution that follows, reaching its climax in the terrible bare-
ness of the last line—these things belong to a mature
Shakespeare, and it has been thought that the passage was
inserted some considerable time after the first acting of the
play. That guess may be correct, yet the authority of the
speech is something we shall meet again in Part III.

A PLAY OF BATTLES

This last Part has a concentrated power that can make it
highly impressive in the theatre. It is a play of battles, yet
with manifest skill the dramatist avoids a sense of repetition.
The first, at Wakefield, is a Lancastrian victory: first we see
Young Clifford's murder of the boy Rutland, the young son of
York, and then the formal mockery and elaborate killing of
York himself. Queen Margaret and Clifford will not at once
dispatch their great enemy. They make him stand on a molehill, in mockery of the height he aspired to; they put a paper
crown upon his head; and Margaret shows him a napkin
stained with Rutland's blood. York is allowed a long speech
of reply, in which he rebukes Margaret for her cruelty and
weeps for Rutland. Then Clifford and Margaret stab him in
turn. This is followed by a Lancastrian defeat at Towton.
Here we see the battle through the King's eyes. First, having
been chidden from the field by the Queen, he takes his stand
on a molehill (as York was forced to do after Wakefield) and
shows his envy of the simple countryman's life, patterned

8. *advised* wise   9. *chair-days* when you ought to be at ease in your chair   10. *virginal* of virgins   11. *reclaims* subdues

according to the seasons, yielding peacefully to the years as
they go, solaced with plain comforts beyond a king's reach:

> O God! methinks it were a happy life
> To be no better than a homely swain;[12]
> To sit upon a hill, as I do now,
> To carve out dials quaintly, point by point,[13]
> Thereby to see the minutes how they run—
> How many makes the hour full complete,
> How many hours brings about the day,
> How many days will finish up the year,
> How many years a mortal man may live.
> When this is known, then to divide the times—
> So many hours must I tend my flock;
> So many hours must I take my rest;
> So many hours must I contemplate;
> So many hours must I sport myself;
> So many days my ewes have been with young;
> So many weeks ere the poor fools will ean;[14]
> So many years ere I shall shear the fleece:
> So minutes, hours, days, months, and years,
> Pass'd over to the end they were created,
> Would bring white hairs unto a quiet grave.
>
> (II.v.21–40)

But in a moment there enters a son that has killed his father
because they have been fighting on opposite sides in the battle, and then a father that has killed his son. The three characters do not speak to each other: they engage in a shared
ritual utterance which voices lamentation for the war's destruction. This passage has the formal nature of drama
around 1590—profoundly animated, however, by a sympathy with human loss. It shows, moreover, that Henry's envy
for the simple countryman has no basis in fact: the war has
brought chaos into every man's family. Then our attention is
turned to the fighting itself, with the Yorkists triumphant.
Clifford is mortally wounded. The three sons of York find
him at the point of death: he dies as they begin to mock him,
and their frustrated desire for verbal revenge, and for the
blow that severs life, stands in antithesis to the achieved
mockery and killing of York at Wakefield. And we see the
war growing more savage. The sons of York hurling their
taunts at a dead body reveal a special barbarity as well as
grim comedy.

In the third and fourth acts of the play there is no open

12. *swain* rustic   13. *carve...point* cut out a sundial on the turf   14. *ean* bring forth
young

battle, but in turn the two sides win tactical advantages through each other's mistakes. The King is captured by the Yorkists; Edward, his father's successor as Duke of York, falls into political error in marrying Lady Grey, an obscure but attractive widow, instead of the French King's sister to whom he had sent the powerful Earl of Warwick as an ambassador of love; Margaret through this wins help from France and from the indignant Warwick; Edward is captured by the Lancastrians, but quickly escapes; he rallies the Yorkist armies, captures Henry again. Then in the last act the formal battles are resumed, and again there is skilful variation in the ways they are presented. At Barnet, Warwick is killed in a Yorkist victory, and his body is quietly borne off by his supporters. At Tewkesbury, Margaret and her son Prince Edward are captured: Edward of York with his brothers Clarence and Gloucester stab the boy to death when he displays courage. The incident, recalling the boy Rutland's death at Wakefield, is no mere repetition of that. Rutland's death was certain as the revengeful Clifford faced him: the boy begged for mercy. Prince Edward's death is unexpected, brutally casual: he has for his killers words of confident rebuke. The play ends with Gloucester's murder of Henry VI in the Tower and then with Edward of York, now Edward IV, rejoicing in his possession of the crown:

> Sound drums and trumpets. Farewell, sour annoy!
> For here, I hope, begins our lasting joy.

(V.vii.45–6)

But the audience knew that the reign of Richard of Gloucester, as Richard III, was not far away; and before long Shakespeare was to use that reign for one of the most assured plays of his earlier career. We have seen that 2 and 3 *Henry VI* are at their most interesting when irony is most evident. Here at the end the irony is prominent, dependent not merely on the audience's knowledge of the ensuing history but on the feebleness of 'I hope' in Edward's proclamation of felicity.

Shakespeare was to penetrate, in his later years, far deeper into human suffering, affection, aspiration, and far deeper also into the mystery of things. But the writer of 2 and 3 *Henry VI* was already a dramatist of major stature in England. Only Christopher Marlowe could compare with him.

Imagery in *King John*

Caroline F.E. Spurgeon

Caroline F.E. Spurgeon explains Shakespeare's extensive imagery of the body and body parts in *King John*, unlike the imagery of all other history plays except *Henry VIII*. Spurgeon argues that the vigorous images of most of the characters convey vitality, which is good, in contrast to the images of the king, which negate life and emphasize his evil nature. Caroline F.E. Spurgeon was professor emerita of English literature at the University of London.

King John, from the point of view of imagery, stands quite apart from the series of York and Lancaster plays. The proportion of subjects of the images is markedly different, and they seem to me to play as a whole a much more dominating part in creating and sustaining atmosphere, than is the case in any other "history" play.

IMAGES OF THE BODY

The images in themselves are in many ways remarkable, and noticeably vivid. The dominating symbol, which outdominates all others in the play is the body and bodily action. It is so in an entirely different and infinitely more imaginative way than in *Coriolanus*, where certain functions or persons in the state are rather weariesomely and perfunctorily compared with various parts of the body. Here one feels, on the contrary, that the poet's imagination was intensely and brilliantly alive, dancing with fire and energy like Philip Faulconbridge[1] himself, and a great part of the extraordinary vigour and vividness of the images is due to the fact that Shakespeare seems to have thought more continuously and definitely than usual of certain outstanding emotions and themes in the play in terms of a person with bodily charac-

---

1. in the play the bastard half brother of Robert Faulconbridge

teristics and bodily movement. It is not possible, especially in a play like *King John,* where Shakespeare's mind is full of a bodily symbol, entirely to separate images of body and bodily action from those of personification, for quite a number might equally well be classified under either heading. In such cases I usually put the image under "Personification" when that seems the most striking aspect, and under "Body" when the special movement appears accentuated.

For the only time in a play of Shakespeare's, images of nature or animals do not head, or almost head, the list, but take definitely the second and third place; by far the greatest number in *King John* are these personifications, reinforced by the large group coming under body or bodily action, making seventy-one listed images in all under these two headings.

The two great protagonists, France and England, the fate that befalls them under the guises of fortune, war and death; the emotions and qualities called into play by the clash of their contending desires: grief, sorrow, melancholy, displeasure, amazement, commodity; the besieged city of Angiers; all these, and other entities or abstractions, are seen by Shakespeare—many of them repeatedly—as *persons;* angry, proud, contemptuous, saucy, indignant, smooth-faced, surly and wanton; sinning, suffering, repenting, kissing, winking, wrestling, resisting, whirling, hurrying, feasting, drinking, bragging, frowning, and grinning. If one looks at it from this angle, one sees that Shakespeare has painted, as a kind of illumination or decorative marginal gloss to the play, a series of tiny allegorical pictures, dancing with life and movement, which, far from lessening the vigour of reality, as allegory sometimes does, increase its vividness and poignancy tenfold.

He sees England, here as elsewhere (cf. *R. II,* III.iii.96 and II.iii.92), as a pale-faced woman, with Neptune's arms clipping her about (*K.J.* V.ii.33), or standing with her foot spurning back "the ocean's roaring tides" (II.i.23), the mother of sons who in war, are reluctantly forced to "march upon her gentle bosom" (V.ii.24) and "fright her pale-faced villages" (*R. II,* II.iii.92).

France, on the other hand, in the eyes of Constance, is a "bawd to Fortune and King John" (*K.J.* III.i.60); fortune, who joined with nature to make Arthur great, is corrupted, changed and sins with John, and has taken France with her golden hand and led her on "to tread down fair respect and sovereignty." The besieged city, the centre of their tussle in the early scenes, is thought of throughout as a *person*—a woman—engirdled with a waist of stone, whose brows, ribs, eyes, cheeks, and bosom are referred to, and of whom the adjectives resisting, contemptuous, winking and saucy are used (II.i.38, 215, 225, 384, 410).

And war is dominant throughout, a wild and ruthless force, a mighty being with "grappling vigour and rough frown" (III.i.104). Little pictures like that of the dogs "bristling" and "snarling" for the "bare-pick'd bone of majesty" (IV.iii.145–50), of the "jolly troop of Huntsmen," "with purpled hands, dyed in the dying slaughter of their foes" (II.i.321–3), of the "storm of war" blown up by Pandulph's[2] breath (V.i.17) or the fire of war rekindled by it (V.ii.83), of John being urged to go forth "and glister like the god of war" (V.i.54), not to hide in his palace, but to run

To meet displeasure farther from the doors,
And grapple with him ere he come so nigh,

(V.i.59–61)

enhance the consciousness of the very present "savage spirit of wild war" (V.ii.74) which broods over all.

Beside war stalks death, a terrible and gruesome figure, as seen by Faulconbridge, his dead chaps lined with steel, the swords of soldiers for his fangs, feasting and "mousing the flesh of men" (II.i.352). Or he appears as the skilful and ever victorious enemy, as Prince Henry sees him, who "having prey'd upon the outward parts," directs his siege

Against the mind, the which he pricks and wounds
With many legions of strange fantasies.

(V.vii.15–18)

To the distraught Constance he is a "carrion monster," the embodiment of all that is most abhorrent and repulsive; yet such is her agony that he is to be longed for and fondled and greeted as a lover, so that she is moved to cry,

O amiable lovely death!
Thou odoriferous stench! sound rottenness!
Arise forth from the couch of lasting night,
. . . . .
Come, grin on me, and I will think thou smilest,
And buss[3] thee as thy wife.

(III.iv.25–35)

It is worth noting that though fortune, war and death are thought of as persons, King John, who is England's greatest

2. in the play, the pope's official emissary   3. *buss* kiss

enemy, is always pictured as a portion of a body only, which seems in some strange way to create of him something specially sinister and horrible. Pandulph thinks of him as represented by the hand which clasps Philip's in seeming amity, and warns the French king that he may

> hold a serpent by the tongue,
> A chafed[4] lion by the mortal[5] paw,
> A fasting tiger safer by the tooth,
> Than keep in peace that hand which thou dost hold.

(III.i.258–261)

He sees that hand dipped in blood, and tells Lewis that when John hears of his approach, if Arthur be not already dead, the king will kill him, and then his people will revolt from him

> And kiss the lips of unacquainted change,
> And pick strong matter of revolt and wrath
> Out of the bloody fingers' ends of John.

(III.iv.166-168)

John thinks of himself as a foot, which, wheresoe'er it treads, finds Arthur as a serpent in his way; and the most terrible and haunting image in the play, which indeed sums up its whole movement, is when his own followers revolt against him as Pandulph prophesied they would, and on the king's bidding them to his presence, Salisbury in their names angrily refuses to

> attend the foot
> That leaves the print of blood where'er it walks.

(IV.iii.25-26)

At the end too, when John gets his deserts, this same feeling of his being but a fragment—a mere counterfeit of humanity—is again emphasised, this time in his own bitter cry that his heart is cracked and burned, that all the shrouds wherewith his life should sail

> Are tuned to one thread, *one little hair*,

(V.vii.54)

and that all his faithful servant and his son are now looking at

> is but a clod
> And module of confounded royalty.[6]

(V.vii.57-58)

This presentation of King John is a good example of one of the varied ways in which Shakespeare—through imagery—

---

4. *chafed* irritated   5. *mortal* deadly   6. *module . . . royalty* specimen of a dead king

often without our conscious recognition of his method, profoundly affects us.

SUBTLE SYMBOLISM

Long before I noticed, in actual statistics, the unusual predominance in this play of images of personification and bodily action, I was generally aware—as all readers must be—of a marked feeling of vigour, life and energy radiating chiefly from Faulconbridge, and of an overpowering feeling of repulsion for John, hardly accounted for by the text. I now believe these two impressions to be partly due to the subtle effect of the curious but quite definite symbolism, which in a play crowded with pictures of dancing, wrestling, whirling human figures, lets us see the king as a portion of a body only, and that portion at times steeped in human blood.

Readers hardly need reminding how extraordinarily vivid are many of the personifications of emotions, such as Constance's two well-known descriptions of grief *(K.J.* III.i.68 and III.iv.93), the later one carrying with it again the same contradictory attraction as in the case of death:

> Grief fills the room up of my absent child
> Lies in his bed, walks up and down with me,
> . . . . .
> Then have I reason to be fond of grief.

John's description of that "surly spirit, melancholy" and his action on the blood, and of "that idiot, laughter" when he is working Hubert to his purposes, is unusual and arresting, as is indeed the whole speech, with its five vivid personifications treading close on each other's heels in the space of sixteen lines (III.iii.31–46). So also Faulconbridge's account of the havoc and flurry wrought among John's few remaining followers when they hear he has yielded to the Pope is unsurpassed in terse pictorial quality:

> And wild amazement hurries up and down
> The little number of your doubtful friends.
>
> (V.i.35–36)

John is very fond of personifications, but then so are many of the characters—Constance, Faulconbridge, Pandulph and Arthur—and this general tendency causes the strangest things to be visualised as persons—the cannon with their "bowels full of wrath" spitting forth "iron indignation" (II.i.210–12); the midnight bell, with "iron tongue and brazen mouth" (III.iii.37); even the insentient iron with which Hubert is to put out Arthur's eyes, and the fire which heats it, the "burning coal" which has not malice in it and is now cold, but which, if revived, will "glow with shame" for his proceedings (IV.i.106–14).

Like *King Lear*, where the symbol of a body torn and shattered is so vivid that it overflows into the ordinary language—the verbs and adjectives of the play—so here, the consciousness of the aspect of a living person, a face, an eye, a brow, a hand, a finger, with characteristic gestures and actions, is almost continuous, and description takes naturally the form of which the following phrases, chosen at random, are a type. They might easily be multiplied two or threefold. "The *coward hand* of France" (II.i.158); "not a word of his But *buffets* better than a *fist* of France" (II.i.464–5); "peace and *fair-faced* league" (II.i.417); "the outward *eye* of fickle France" (II.i.583); "move the *murmuring* lips of discontent" (IV.ii.53); "the *gentle brow* Of true sincerity" (III.i.247); "O, that my *tongue* were in the thunder's mouth!" (III.iv.38); "outface the *brow* Of *bragging* horror" (V.i.49); "the *black brow* of night" (V.vi.17). It is not surprising therefore that we find nearly all the chief emotional themes or moving forces in the play summed up with unforgettable vividness in the little vignette of this type: the selfish motives of the two kings in the Bastard's sketch of

> That smooth-faced gentleman, tickling Commodity;[7]
>
> (II.i.573)

the terrible position Blanch finds herself in with a newly-wed husband in one army and her uncle in the other, in her amazing and haunting picture of being torn asunder in opposite directions:

> Which is the side that I must go withal?
> I am with both: each army hath a hand;
> and in the rage, I having hold of both,
> They whirl asunder and dismember me;
>
> (III.i.327–30)

Constance's grief; Arthur's horror at the red-hot iron; the bewilderment and uncertainty of John's followers (V.i.35); finger tips and footprint; and his mental and physical agony at the end, when forsaken, defeated and dying from a virulent poison which is burning him up internally, making a hell within him, he cries, in answer to his son's query, "How

---

7. *tickling Commodity* flattering self-interest

fares your majesty?"

> Poison'd,—ill fare—dead, forsook, cast off;
> And none of you will bid the winter come
> To thrust his icy fingers in my maw,[8]
>   . . . nor entreat the north
> To make his bleak winds kiss my parched lips
> And comfort me with cold.

(V.vii.34–41)

In *Henry VIII,* so far removed in treatment and spirit from *King John,* the dominating image, curiously enough, is again the body and bodily action, but used in an entirely different way and at a different angle from that in the earlier play. The continuous picture or symbol in the poet's mind is not so much a person displaying certain emotions and characteristics, as a mere physical body in endlessly varied action. Thus I find only four "personifications" in the play, whereas in *King John* I count no less than forty. . . .

In two of the histories we note that the image symbolism quite definitely—in the method of the comedies—contributes atmosphere and quality to the play. Thus in *Henry VIII* the feeling of swift and soaring movement is markedly emphasised, and in *King John,* which in treatment stands out from all the other histories, the very marked and consistent "floating" image brings out the contrast between the surging vigorous life in most of the characters in the play, and the negation of life, which is evil, in the person of the cruel and craven king. It thus heightens immensely the imaginative and poetical effectiveness of the theme.

8. *maw* stomach

APPENDIX A

ENGLISH MONARCHS FROM THE NORMAN CONQUEST THROUGH SHAKESPEARE'S TIME

Editor's Note: The asterisks indicate the kings about whom Shakespeare wrote plays; the numbers indicate the order in which he wrote them. The kings' houses are identified from the time leading up to, during, and following the Wars of the Roses (1455–1485).

1066–1087	William I (the Conqueror)	
1087–1100	William II	
1100–1135	Henry I	
1135–1154	Stephen	
1154–1189	Henry II	
1189–1199	Richard I (the Lionheart)	
1199–1216	John* 6	
1216–1272	Henry III	
1272–1307	Edward I	
1307–1327	Edward II	
1327–1377	Edward III	
1377–1399	Richard II* 5	Lancaster
1399–1413	Henry IV* 7, 8	Lancaster
1413–1422	Henry V* 9	Lancaster
1422–1461 and 1470–1471	Henry VI* 1, 2, 3	Lancaster
1461–1470 and 1471–1483	Edward IV	York
1483	Edward V	York
1483–1485	Richard III* 4	York
1485–1509	Henry VII	Tudor
1509–1547	Henry VIII* 10	Tudor
1547–1553	Edward VI	Tudor
1553–1558	Mary I	Tudor
1558–1603	Elizabeth I	Tudor
1603–1625	James I	Stuart

Appendix B

Genealogical Tables

Table A. The House of Lancaster

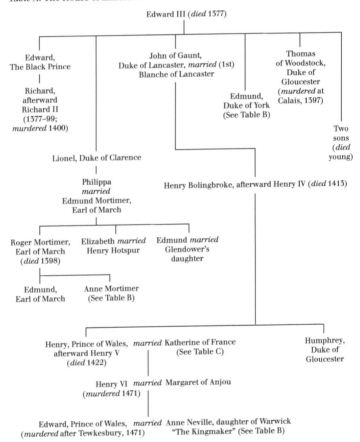

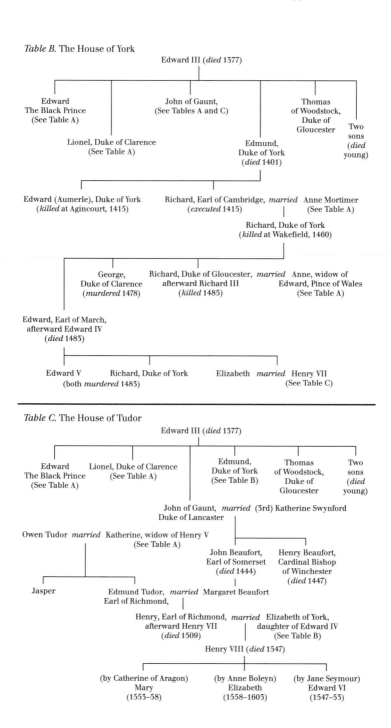

Table B. The House of York

Edward III (*died* 1377)

Edward
The Black Prince
(See Table A)

John of Gaunt,
(See Tables A and C)

Thomas
of Woodstock,
Duke of
Gloucester

Two
sons
(*died
young*)

Lionel, Duke of Clarence
(See Table A)

Edmund,
Duke of York
(*died* 1401)

Edward (Aumerle), Duke of York
(*killed* at Agincourt, 1415)

Richard, Earl of Cambridge, *married* Anne Mortimer
(*executed* 1415)   (See Table A)

Richard, Duke of York
(*killed* at Wakefield, 1460)

George,
Duke of Clarence
(*murdered* 1478)

Richard, Duke of Gloucester, *married* Anne, widow of
afterward Richard III   Edward, Pince of Wales
(*killed* 1485)   (See Table A)

Edward, Earl of March,
afterward Edward IV
(*died* 1483)

Edward V   Richard, Duke of York   Elizabeth *married* Henry VII
(both *murdered* 1483)   (See Table C)

Table C. The House of Tudor

Edward III (*died* 1377)

Edward
The Black Prince
(See Table A)

Lionel, Duke of Clarence
(See Table A)

Edmund,
Duke of York
(See Table B)

Thomas
of Woodstock,
Duke of
Gloucester

Two
sons
(*died
young*)

John of Gaunt, *married* (3rd) Katherine Swynford
Duke of Lancaster

Owen Tudor *married* Katherine, widow of Henry V
(See Table A)

John Beaufort,
Earl of Somerset
(*died* 1444)

Henry Beaufort,
Cardinal Bishop
of Winchester
(*died* 1447)

Jasper

Edmund Tudor, *married* Margaret Beaufort
Earl of Richmond,

Henry, Earl of Richmond, *married* Elizabeth of York,
afterward Henry VII   daughter of Edward IV
(*died* 1509)   (See Table B)

Henry VIII (*died* 1547)

(by Catherine of Aragon)
Mary
(1553–58)

(by Anne Boleyn)
Elizabeth
(1558–1603)

(by Jane Seymour)
Edward VI
(1547–53)

CHRONOLOGY

1557
Shakespeare's parents, John Shakespeare and Mary Arden, marry

1558
Elizabeth I becomes queen of England

1561
Philosopher and statesman Francis Bacon born; advanced as actual writer of Shakespeare's plays by skeptics in modern age

1562
First English participation in New World slave trade from Africa

1564
William Shakespeare born; English dramatist Christopher Marlowe born; Italian painter, sculptor, and architect Michelangelo dies at eighty-eight

1569
John Shakespeare becomes bailiff of Stratford

CA. 1570
Emilia Bassano, daughter of a court musician and suggested real-life dark lady of the Sonnets, born

1572
Ben Jonson, English playwright and poet, born

1576
The Theatre, England's first playhouse, built in London

1577–1580
Sir Francis Drake's first English voyage around the world

1578
Historian and printer Raphael Holinshed publishes *Chronicles of English History to 1575*, source of material for Shakespeare's histories

1582

Shakespeare marries Anne Hathaway

1583

Daughter Susanna born

1584

Sir Walter Raleigh founds Virginia colony on Roanoke Island

1585

Twins Hamnet and Judith born

1587

Execution of Mary, Queen of Scots, by order of Elizabeth I; Marlowe's *Tamburlaine* performed in London

1587–1590

Shakespeare acting and touring

1588

Spanish Armada defeated by British navy, making way for England's ascendancy in world trade and colonization

1591

1 Henry VI

1591–1592

2 and *3 Henry VI*

1592

Plague in London causes closure of theaters; Robert Greene attacks Shakespeare in print, the first known reference to Shakespeare's reputation or work; Galileo proves objects fall at the same rate regardless of their weight, in Pisa

1592–1593

The Comedy of Errors; Sonnets; *Richard III*

1593

Plague in London continues; Marlowe dies in tavern brawl; *Titus Andronicus; The Taming of the Shrew; The Two Gentlemen of Verona; Love's Labour's Lost; Venus and Adonis* published

1594

Lord Chamberlain's Men, Shakespeare's acting company, formed; *The Rape of Lucrece* published

1594–1595

A Midsummer Night's Dream; Romeo and Juliet; Richard II

1595–1596

The Merchant of Venice

1596

Shakespeare applies for and receives coat of arms in his father's name, achieves gentleman status; Hamnet Shakespeare dies; *King John*

1597

Shakespeare buys New Place, property in Stratford that becomes his family's home; *1 Henry IV*

1598

The Theatre torn down; timbers used for new Globe; *2 Henry IV; Much Ado About Nothing*

1599

Globe theater opens; *Henry V; As You Like It; Julius Caesar; The Merry Wives of Windsor;* "The Passionate Pilgrim" published

1600–1601

Twelfth Night; Hamlet; Troilus and Cressida

1601

John Shakespeare dies; "The Phoenix and the Turtle"

1602

Shakespeare buys land at Stratford; *Othello*

1603

Bubonic plague strikes London; Elizabeth I dies; James I becomes king of England; English conquest of Ireland; Lord Chamberlain's Men become King's Men; *All's Well That Ends Well*

1604

Measure for Measure

1605

Repression of Catholics and Puritans; Gunpowder Plot to kill James I and members of Parliament; Shakespeare invests in Stratford tithes; world's first newspaper begins publication in Antwerp

1606

Visit by the king of Denmark; Ben Jonson's *Volpone; King Lear; Macbeth*

1607

Jamestown, Virginia, founded; daughter Susanna marries Dr. John Hall

1607–1609
Antony and Cleopatra; Coriolanus; Timon of Athens (unfinished); *Pericles*

1608
Plague in London; King's Men acquire Blackfriars theater; granddaughter Elizabeth Hall born; Mary Arden Shakespeare dies

1609
Sonnets and "A Lover's Complaint" published by Thomas Thorpe, an edition believed unauthorized; Johannes Kepler proves planetary orbits are elliptical

1610
Cymbeline

1610–1611
The Winter's Tale

1611
The Maydenhead of the first musicke that ever was printed for the Virginalls, first book of keyboard music in England; King James Bible published; Shakespeare contributes to highway bill, repairing roads between Stratford and London; *The Tempest*

1612
Shakespeare's brother Gilbert dies

1612–1613
Henry VIII

1613
The Globe burns down; Shakespeare's brother Richard dies; Shakespeare buys house in Blackfriars area; Galileo says Copernicus was right; Vatican arrests Galileo in 1616

1615
Miguel de Cervantes completes *Don Quixote* in Spain

1616
Daughter Judith marries Thomas Quiney; Shakespeare dies

1623
Anne Hathaway Shakespeare dies; actors Condell and Heminge publish Shakespeare's collected plays in a single volume known as the First Folio

FOR FURTHER RESEARCH

ABOUT WILLIAM SHAKESPEARE AND THE HISTORIES

Peter Alexander, *Shakespeare's Life and Art*. London: James Nisbet, 1939.

M.C. Bradbrook, *Shakespeare the Craftsman: The Clark Lectures 1968*. London: Cambridge University Press, 1969.

John C. Bromley, *The Shakespearean Kings*. Boulder: Colorado Associated University Press, 1971.

Ivor Brown, *How Shakespeare Spent the Day*. New York: Hill and Wang, 1963.

Victor L. Cahn, *Shakespeare the Playwright: A Companion to the Complete Tragedies, Histories, Comedies, and Romances*. London: Praeger, 1996.

Lily Campbell, *Shakespeare's "Histories."* San Marino, CA: The Huntington Library, 1947.

Samuel Taylor Coleridge, *Shakespearean Criticism* (1811–1834), ed. T.M. Raysor. Cambridge, MA: Harvard University Press, 1930.

Hardin Craig and David Berington, *An Introduction to Shakespeare*. Rev. ed. Glenview, IL: Scott, Foresman, 1975.

Edward Dowden, *Shakespeare: A Critical Study of His Mind and Art*. New York: Harper & Brothers, 1880.

Gareth and Barbara Lloyd Evans, *The Shakespeare Companion*. New York: Charles Scribner's Sons, 1978.

Levi Fox, *The Shakespeare Handbook*. Boston: G.K. Hall, 1987.

Harley Granville-Barker and G.B. Harrison, eds., *A Companion to Shakespeare Studies*. New York: Cambridge University Press, 1934.

Alice Griffin, ed., *The Sources of Ten Shakespearean Plays*. New York: Thomas Y. Crowell, 1966.

Dennis Kay, *Shakespeare: His Life, Work, and Era.* New York: William Morrow, 1992.

Victor Kiernan, *Shakespeare: Poet and Citizen.* New York: Verso, 1993.

Sidney Lee, *A Life of William Shakespeare.* New York: Dover, 1968.

John Middleton Murry, *Shakespeare.* New York: Harcourt, Brace, 1936.

Dorothy Ogburn and Charlton Ogburn Jr., *Shake-speare: The Man Behind the Name.* New York: William Morrow, 1962.

H.M. Richmond, *Shakespeare's Political Plays.* Gloucester, MA: Peter Smith, 1967.

A.L. Rowse, *Shakespeare the Man.* New York: Harper & Row, 1973.

———, *What Shakespeare Read and Thought.* New York: Coward, McCall & Geoghagan, 1981.

A.L. Rowse and John Hedgecoe, *Shakespeare's Land: A Journey Through the Landscape of Elizabethan England.* San Francisco: Chronicle Books, 1987.

Samuel Schoenbaum, *William Shakespeare: A Documentary Life.* New York: Oxford University Press in association with The Scholar Press, 1975.

Edith Sitwell, *A Notebook on William Shakespeare.* Boston: Beacon Press, 1948.

Logan Pearsall Smith, *On Reading Shakespeare.* New York: Harcourt, Brace, 1933.

Theodore Spencer, *Shakespeare and the Nature of Man: Lowell Lectures, 1942.* 2nd ed. London: Collier-Macmillan, 1949.

Caroline F.E. Spurgeon, *Shakespeare's Imagery and What It Tells Us.* 1935. Reprint, New York: Cambridge University Press, 1987.

ABOUT ELIZABETHAN THEATERS AND ENGLISH HISTORY

Joseph Quincy Adams, *Shakespearean Playhouses.* New York: Houghton Mifflin, 1917.

Maurice Ashley, *Great Britain to 1688.* Ann Arbor: University of Michigan Press, 1961.

Arthur Bryant, *Spirit of England.* London: William Collins, 1982.

Elizabeth Burton, *The Pageant of Elizabethan England.* New York: Charles Scribner's Sons, 1958.

John Cannon and Ralph Griffiths, *The Oxford Illustrated History of the British Monarchy.* New York: Oxford University Press, 1988.

Will and Ariel Durant, *The Age of Reason Begins: A History of European Civilization in the Period of Shakespeare, Bacon, Montaigne, Rembrandt, Galileo, and Descartes: 1558–1658.* Vol. 7 of *The Story of Civilization.* New York: Simon and Schuster, 1961.

Alfred Harbage, *Shakespeare's Audience.* New York: Columbia University Press, 1941.

G.B. Harrison, *Elizabethan Plays and Players.* Ann Arbor: University of Michigan Press, 1956.

C. Walter Hodges, *The Battlement Garden: Britain from the Wars of the Roses to the Age of Shakespeare.* New York: Houghton Mifflin/Clarion Books, 1979.

A.V. Judges, *The Elizabethan Underworld.* New York: Octagon Books, 1965.

Gweyneth Morgan, *Life in a Medieval Village.* Minneapolis: Lerner, 1982.

A.R. Myers, *England in the Late Middle Ages.* Middlesex, England: Penguin Books, 1971.

Walter Raleigh, ed., *Shakespeare's England.* 2 vols. Oxford: Clarendon Press, 1916.

Conyers Read, *The Tudors: Personalities and Practical Politics in Sixteenth-Century England.* New York: Henry Holt, 1936.

Shakespeare and the Theatre. London: Members of the Shakespeare Association of London, 1927. (A series of papers by a variety of critics.)

Doris Mary Stenton, *English Society in the Early Middle Ages, 1066–1307.* Middlesex, England: Penguin Books, 1963.

E.M.W. Tillyard, *The Elizabethan World Picture.* New York: Macmillan, 1943.

George Macaulay Trevelyan, *The Age of Shakespeare and the Stuart Period.* Vol. 2 of *Illustrated English Social History.* London: Longmans, Green, 1950.

———, *History of England: From the Earliest Times to the Reformation.* Vol. 1. Garden City, NY: Doubleday Anchor Books, 1953.

ORGANIZATIONS TO CONTACT

The following Shakespeare societies have information or publications available to interested readers. The descriptions are derived from materials provided by the organizations. This list was compiled as of the date of publication. Names and phone numbers are subject to change.

International Shakespeare Association (ISA)
The Shakespeare Center
Henley Street
Stratford upon Avon, Warwickshire, England
CV37 6 QW
phone: 44 1789 204016
fax: 44 1789 296083

The association gathers and disseminates information on Shakespearean research, publications, translations, and performances. It maintains and circulates a diary of future performances, conferences, opportunities for graduate work, and educational experiments relating to Shakespeare's works.

Shakespeare Oxford Society (SOS)
Greenridge Pk.
7D Taggart Dr.
Nashua, NH 03060-5591
Leonard Deming, Membership Chairman
phone: (603) 888-1453 or (508) 349-2087
e-mail: business@shakespeare.oxford.im.com

The society provides information on research into history of the Elizabethan period of English literature. It explores and attempts to verify evidence bearing on the authorship of works attributed to Shakespeare, particularly evidence indicating that Edward de Vere, the seventeenth earl of Oxford, was the author; it searches for original manuscripts in England to support its theories. It conducts research and educational programs; maintains a speakers bureau; publishes brochures, pamphlets, and the quarterly *Shakespeare Oxford Society Newsletter;* and holds an annual fall conference.

WORKS BY WILLIAM SHAKESPEARE

Editor's Note: Many of the dates on this list are approximate. Since manuscripts identified with the date of writing do not exist, scholars have determined the most accurate available date, either of the writing or of the first production of each play.

1 Henry VI (1591)

2 and *3 Henry VI* (1591–1592)

The Comedy of Errors; Richard III; Sonnets (1592–1593)

Titus Andronicus; The Taming of the Shrew: The Two Gentlemen of Verona; Love's Labour's Lost; publication of *Venus and Adonis* (1593)

Publication of *The Rape of Lucrece* (1594)

A Midsummer Night's Dream; Romeo and Juliet; Richard II (1594–1595)

The Merchant of Venice (1595–1596)

King John (1596)

1 Henry IV (1597)

2 Henry IV; Much Ado About Nothing (1598)

Henry V; As You Like It; Julius Caesar; The Merry Wives of Windsor; publication of "The Passionate Pilgrim" (1599)

Twelfth Night; Hamlet; Troilus and Cressida (1600–1601)

"The Phoenix and the Turtle" (1601)

Othello (1602)

All's Well That Ends Well (1603)

Measure for Measure (1604)

King Lear; Macbeth (1606)

Antony and Cleopatra; Coriolanus; Timon of Athens (unfinished); *Pericles* (1607–1609)

Sonnets and "A Lover's Complaint," first published by Thomas Thorpe (1609)

Cymbeline (1610)

The Winter's Tale (1610–1611)

The Tempest (1611)

Henry VIII (1612–1613)

INDEX

acting companies, 16, 19, 64
    see also Lord Chamberlain's Men
All's Well That Ends Well, 25
Antony and Cleopatra, 25
Aristotle, 45, 47
Armada, Spanish, 42, 43
As You Like It, 23
Aubrey, John, 16, 17

Bacon, Francis, 28
Bamber, Linda, 57
Bassano, Emilia, 19
Becker, George J., 64
Betterton, Thomas, 68
Bible, 15
Birmingham Repertory Theatre, 69, 162
Book of Common Prayer, 15
Book of Martyrs (Foxe), 18
Brooke, Tucker, 42
Brown, John Russell, 149
Burbage, James, 17, 20, 22, 26
Burbage, Richard, 20, 64

Calderwood, James L., 112
Calvin, John, 97
Campbell, Lily B., 40
Charlton, H.B., 43–44, 132
Chronicles (Hall), 18
Chronicles (Holinshed), 18, 140
Cibber, Colley, 68, 69
Coleridge, Samuel Taylor, 41
Condell, Henry, 20, 28
Coriolanus, 25, 70
Cranmer, Thomas, 18
Cymbeline, 27, 40

Daniel, Samuel, 85
Dethick, William, 22
Dowden, Edward, 99

Elizabeth I (queen of England), 15, 17, 18, 38, 140
    death of, 24
    feeling of people for, 48

English Chronicle Play, The (Schelling), 41
English History in Shakespeare (Marriott), 44

Falstaff, Sir John, 21, 66, 127, 132, 139
    as aspect of Hal's character development, 105, 114
    as clown, 54, 105, 110–12, 114
    on honor, 111, 113, 121–22
    and soldier, 65, 107
    and comedy of aging, 135
    contrasted with Hotspur, 106
    and Elizabethan acting style, 68
    and Gad's Hill Incident, 107–109
    and Hotspur/Hal duel, 112
    impudence of, 130
    and miscalculation of Hal, 133
    as representative of common folk, 136, 148
    and rejection by Henry, 134, 140, 143, 150
    theatricality of, 109, 122
Famous Victories of Henry the Fifth (Anon.), 116, 140
Fergusson, Francis, 139
Field, Richard, 19
First Folio, 28, 40, 160, 161
Foxe, John, 18
Froissart, Sir John, 85

Garrick, David, 67
Goldman, Michael, 63
Greene, Robert, 19, 161
Gupta, S.C. Sen, 79

Hall, Edward, 18, 38, 45, 87
Hamlet, 23, 65, 87, 148
Harrison, G.B., 21, 23, 27
Heminge, John, 20, 28
Henry IV, 20, 21, 41, 55, 115
    Part One, 50, 69, 85, 133
        chivalric code of, 54
        contrasts in, 121–22
        and irony, 50

189